BAD BOYS

OF THE

BLACK HILLS

...And Some Wild Women, Too

BY BARBARA FIFER

INTRODUCTION BY JERRY BRYANT

FARCOUNTRY
PRESS

HELENA, MONTANA

ACKNOWLEDGMENTS

Besides the authors whose works I studied, I am very grateful to Jerry Bryant, research curator and archaeologist of Adams Museum in Deadwood, South Dakota, for catching where my research and understanding failed and for sharing his enthusiastic interest in this place during its most flamboyant era; to Gerry Robinson, for help with Northern Cheyenne history; to Caroline Patterson and John Thomas for sharp but thoughtful editing; and to Shirley Machonis for entering into the spirit of nineteenth-century book design.

Cover: From left to right, James Butler "Wild Bill" Hickok, John B. "Texas Jack" Omohundro, and William F. "Buffalo Bill" Cody.
MCCRACKEN RESEARCH LIBRARY, BUFFALO BILL HISTORICAL CENTER P.69.2179.

Back cover: Deadwood in 1877, a year after its founding.
NEBRASKA STATE HISTORICAL SOCIETY RG2573 PH 31.

ISBN 10: 1-56037-435-7
ISBN 13: 978-1-56037-435-0

© 2008 by Farcountry Press
Text © 2008 by Barbara Fifer

For more information on our books, write Farcountry Press, P.O. Box 5630, Helena, MT 59604; call (800) 821-3874; or visit www.farcountrypress.com.

Library of Congress Cataloging-in-Publication Data

Fifer, Barbara.
  Bad boys of the Black Hills : and some wild women, too / by Barbara Fifer.
    p. cm.
  ISBN-13: 978-1-56037-435-0 (softcover)
  ISBN-10: 1-56037-435-7 (softcover)
  1. Black Hills (S.D. and Wyo.)--History--19th century--Anecdotes. 2. Black Hills (S.D. and Wyo.)--Social life and customs--19th century--Anecdotes. 3. Frontier and pioneer life--Black Hills (S.D. and Wyo.)--Anecdotes. 4. Black Hills (S.D. and Wyo.)--Biography. 5. Pioneers--Black Hills (S.D. and Wyo.)--Biography. 6. Outlaws--Black Hills (S.D. and Wyo.)--Biography. 7. Brigands and robbers--Black Hills (S.D. and Wyo.)--Biography. 8. Rogues and vagabonds--Black Hills (S.D. and Wyo.)--Biography. 9. Prostitutes--Black Hills (S.D. and Wyo.)--Biography. I. Title.
  F657.B6F545 2008
  978.3'9020922--dc22

                              2008018621

Created, produced, and designed in the United States.
Printed in Canada.

16   15   14   13   12   3   4   5   6   7

For Tomala and Judy, my Albany cousins,
with thanks for their friendship and love

But lust for gold all conscience kills in man,
"Gold in the Black Hills, gold!" the cry arose and ran
From lip to lip, as flames from tree to tree
Leap till the forest is one fiery sea,
And through the country surged that hot unrest
Which thirst for riches wakens in the breast.

—ELLA WHEELER WILCOX, FROM "CUSTER"

DEADWOOD-TO-CHEYENNE ROADS

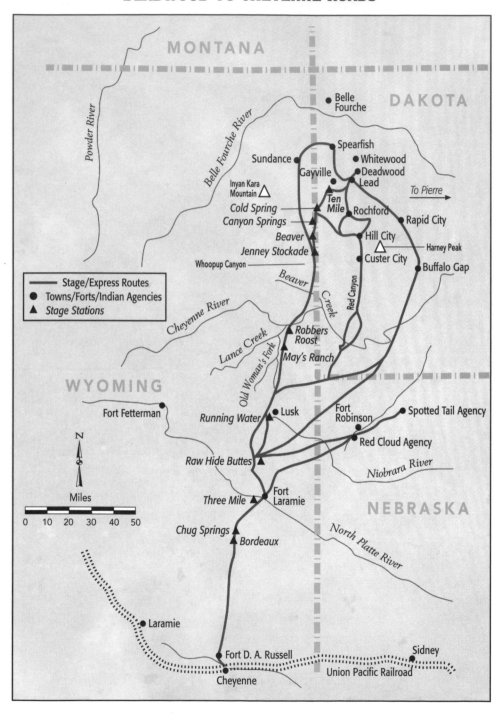

MONTANA

DAKOTA

Powder River

Belle Fourche River

Belle Fourche

Spearfish

Sundance

Gayville

Whitewood

Deadwood

Lead

To Pierre

Inyan Kara Mountain

Cold Spring

Ten Mile

Rochford

Rapid City

Canyon Springs

Beaver

Hill City

Harney Peak

Jenney Stockade

Custer City

Whoopup Canyon

Buffalo Gap

Beaver Creek

Red Canyon

Cheyenne River

Lance Creek

Robbers Roost

May's Ranch

Old Woman's Fork

WYOMING

Fort Fetterman

Running Water

Lusk

Fort Robinson

Spotted Tail Agency

Red Cloud Agency

Niobrara River

Raw Hide Buttes

Three Mile

Fort Laramie

NEBRASKA

Chug Springs

Bordeaux

North Platte River

Laramie

Fort D. A. Russell

Sidney

Cheyenne

Union Pacific Railroad

Legend
— Stage/Express Routes
● Towns/Forts/Indian Agencies
▲ Stage Stations

N

Miles
0 10 20 30 40 50

TABLE OF CONTENTS

PREFACE — ix

INTRODUCTION — x

TIMELINE — xiii

CHAPTER ONE

THE MAIN ROAD, A TREASURE COACH & BROTHELS

Metropolises at Road's Ends — 1

Paying by the Pinch — 5

Black Hills Trail — 5

Concord Coaches — 7

The Monitor — 8

"Rescue of the Deadwood Stage" — 9

Pony Expresses Everywhere — 11

Brothels Along the Stage Road — 12

Wyatt Earp — 13

CHAPTER TWO

LAW-ABIDING BAD BOYS

George Armstrong Custer — 16

The Earliest Miners — 20

James Butler "Wild Bill" Hickok — 23

Samuel Fields — 34

John B. "Johnny" Owens — 35

Scott "Quick Shot" Davis — 37

Vigilantes — 38

CHAPTER THREE

KILLERS INTENTIONAL & NOT

Tom Milligan — 42

William F. "Persimmon Bill" Chambers — 44

H. E. "Stuttering" Brown — 46

Jack McCall — 48

Harry "Sam" Young — 51

Richard "Banjo Dick" Brown — 53

Boone May — 54

Two Murder/Suicides in the Name of Love — 57
CHARLEY WILSON & KITTY CLIDE — 57
SAM CURLEY & KITTY LEROY — 58

William (Bill) Gay — 59

CHAPTER FOUR

ROBBERS, RUSTLERS & PLAIN OLD THIEVES

Triple Robberies & Some Murders — 61
ROBERT "LITTLE REDDY" MCKIMIE — 62
BILL BEVANS — 65
CLARK PELTON — 66
SAMUEL S. "LAUGHING SAM" HARTMAN — 67
DUNC BLACKBURN & JAMES WALL — 67
JAMES WALL SPARES AN OLD FRIEND — 71

Sam Bass & Joel Collins — 72

Jack Bowman & Jack Bowman — 73

Prescott Webb — 74

Cornelius "Lame Johnny" Donahue — 75

Frank Warren — 78

Whoopup Canyon Robbery — 79
JOHN H. "JOHNNY" BROWN — 79
GEORGE W. KEATING & ORBEAN DAVIS — 80
CHARLES HENRY BORRIS — 80
CHARLEY ROSS — 81

The Monitor is Robbed at Canyon Springs — 82
THOMAS JEFFERSON "DUCK" GOODALE — 85
WILLIAM "BILLY" MANSFIELD & ARCHIE MCLAUGHLIN — 86
AL SPEARS — 86
CHARLES CAREY — 87
FRANK MCBRIDE — 87
ANDY "RED CLOUD" GOUCH — 88
THE MONITOR'S FATE — 88

Frank K. Towle — 89

William "Curly" Grimes — 91

Harry Longabaugh — 92

The Wild Bunch Fails in Belle Fourche — 97

CHAPTER FIVE

ENTERTAINMENTS HIGH & LOW

The Game of Faro — 99

Chuck-A-Luck — 100

Not-So-Soiled Doves — 101

"Hit it, Perfessor!" — 102

The Gem & Other Variety Theaters — 103

Jack Langrishe & Company — 106

Words for Wicked Women — 109

Monday Afternoons for Shopping — 110

A Drink on the House — 110

Ace Moyer, Con Moyer & "Big Steve" Long — 111

Adolph Cuny & Jules Coffey — 113

Porter's Hotel — 115

Al Swearingen — 116

CHAPTER SIX

FRAIL SISTERS OF THE FRONTIER

Cats for the Houses — 120

Georgia Dow — 122

Martha "Calamity Jane" Cannary — 123

Kitty Austin (Arnold) — 132

Little Frank — 132

Mollie Johnson — 133

Madam Mustache — 134

Charlotte Shepherd — 135

Pearl Leopold — 137

Fannie Hill — 138

Dora Dufran — 139

CHAPTER SEVEN

MORE WILD WOMEN

Lurline Monte Verde — 142

Henrico Livingstone — 145

Inez Sexton — 146

Madam Bulldog — 146

Mrs. Brennan — 149

Mrs. Hayes — 149

Sue Neill — 150

Maggie Laughlin — 151

Poker Alice Tubbs — 152

CHAPTER EIGHT

TALL-TALE TELLERS

William F. "Buffalo Bill" Cody — 156

Captain Jack Crawford — 159

Dime Novels — 163

Deadwood Dick — 165

Nat Love — 167

Edward L. Wheeler — 171

Edward Zane Carroll Judson — 173

Prentiss Ingraham — 177

BIBLIOGRAPHY — 179

INDEX — 181

PREFACE

istory doesn't provide very much solid information on many of the Black Hills bad boys and wild women who continue to fascinate us. Few left photographs, some had only their nicknames recorded while others left a string of aliases, and the sole outstanding (usually horrific) event of their lives was recorded only in newspaper accounts or the memoirs of others.

Some people described here are among the most famous figures of the Wild West, but their biographies became entangled in myths, including tales they themselves created, even while they were living.

Usually the gold rush stories focus solely on outlaws, or lawmen, or shady women, or respectable ladies in a single volume. I wanted to bring them all together, as they existed in the small towns of Deadwood and its satellites in Dakota Territory, and along the territory's lifeline to Cheyenne, Wyoming. Here you will find upstanding lawmen who were willing, even eager, to break the law when they believed that it served justice; gunmen who were good with their weapons, and some who were not so; robbers who did everything wrong and others whose gangs functioned like well-oiled machines; women who made their livings beyond the pale of respectability but not in the bawdy houses; and women who coped with rough frontier living while adhering to Victorian mores.

Working within time and budget constraints, I've turned to the works of western historians, regional historians, cultural history specialists, and some memoirs of Deadwood residents. I've also looked a bit into what people did to enjoy their ill-gotten gains, or to make a new life that emulated part of that left behind. With deep gratitude to those whose works I read, I recommend that interested readers turn to the bibliography to learn more. And I hope I haven't created new errors of interpretation during this fascinating process.

— *Barbara Fifer*

INTRODUCTION

BY JERRY BRYANT

Adams Museum and House, Black Hills, South Dakota

In this volume, Barbara Fifer dares to venture away from the common mold used to study history. Although she pays tribute to all the standard legends and characters, such as Wild Bill Hickok and Calamity Jane, she quickly moves on to examine lesser-known characters who contributed to the rich and storied heritage of the Black Hills. The book is aptly titled *Bad Boys of the Black Hills...And Some Wild Women, Too*; a good examination of the area's history will show you that those individual are the grist that made the mill turn in early Black Hills settlements.

It is nothing short of astounding that Deadwood, a small mining camp clinging to the edges of a narrow gulch in Dakota Territory, achieved the acclaim it acquired in the final twenty-four years of the nineteenth century. Much of its fame was based on two social engines: economics and transportation. From an economic standpoint, there had to be enough gold in the Black Hills to support any number of gamblers, dance hall girls, prostitutes, cutthroats, road agents, and general desperadoes. Without the merchants, whores, and whoremongers and the revenue they generated, all the businesses would have folded after the first major stagecoach robbery. Most importantly, their customers would have moved on to the next El Dorado. This economic activity was especially important because Deadwood did not continue as a mining center after the placer gold ran out. The centers for hard rock and quartz mining were everywhere in the Black Hills but Deadwood.

Instead, the mining camp served as the terminus for all incoming goods. Deadwood was the end of the line for all bull trains, mule trains, and railroad freight. It was a place where everyone had to get off the bus—a sailor town in the dead center of America. And many of the folks who lived in Deadwood found themselves there precisely because it was the end of the line.

Founded the year before, Deadwood in 1877 was frantically mining, doing business, building the town, and receiving more emigrants on its way to a peak population of about 10,000. LIBRARY OF CONGRESS, ‡LC USZ62-23301.

Gamblers and fortune tellers, telegraphers and has-been lawyers, steamboat captains and poets all coexisted in Deadwood. There, they became the planners, financiers, railroad builders, and practical dreamers. In the Black Hills, Deadwood had the first telegraph, the first telephones, and some of the earliest electric streetlights. But Deadwood also had Al Swearingen and the Gem Theatre, Frenchy the Bottle Fiend, Madame Bulldog, Madame Moustache, Madame Molly Johnston, and Samuel Fields—whose fear of being lynched made him run and hide at the jail any time mischief was afoot. It is to these characters that Fifer pays the greatest tribute.

Considering the actual size of the Black Hills, which is only about 1.2 million acres, one cannot help but be amazed by the volumes of historical, fictional, and scientific literature that have been written about the area. Who would have known this small mountain range in the midst of the North American plains would have such an impact on America and on the world as a whole? Prior to the HBO® series *Deadwood*, you would have been hard-pressed to find a European adult who had heard of Sol Star or Dan Dougherty, while just about every person in the modern world knew of Wild Bill Hickok and Calamity Jane. But because of this series, those names and others—including Seth Bullock, Preacher Smith, and Al Swearingen—are being discussed in the Americas, Europe, and even in the Far East.

The demand for more historic information on Black Hills characters has never been higher. While the series is a work of art that is superbly directed and acted, it merely scratches the surface of Black Hills history. That scratch, however, has caused people all over the world to ask more questions and to seek more information. Some of the area's stories have already been told and are waiting to be rediscovered, which is why, I suppose, they call it *research*. But for me, the most thrilling aspect of interest in the area's wild and colorful history is that the story of the Black Hills can never be fully told. There will always be room for another researcher to dig up and turn over new material.

In Fifer's book I renewed my friendship with a plethora of characters I had not thought of in some time, including Richard Bullock, an honest-to-goodness hero stagecoach guard, and Henrico Livingstone, the medical clairvoyant fortune teller and lady miner. The author takes readers to the Hog Ranch, where the sporting ladies often wore soldier's uniforms or buckskins, and sometimes both. She also brings to light just how multi-layered Black Hills history is: In a single Deadwood instant, miners drive shafts; an ox train hauls a steam-driven sawmill up Main Street; a saloon keeper polishes a glass; a young prostitute is shot by her lover; silver is discovered in another, nearby gulch; and a newspaper editor holds a galley proof up to the light before starting the day's run. In the end, Ms. Fifer's book sustains that enthusiasm, captures a true aspect of the Black Hills gold rush, and leaves you longing for more. ⇥

Jerry Bryant is a research curator and historical archaeologist at the Adams Museum and House in the Black Hills of South Dakota.

BLACK HILLS TIMELINE

1861

- Dakota Territory formed, including present South Dakota, Wyoming, Montana, and North Dakota.

1864

- Montana Territory created and removed from Dakota Territory.

1868

- Wyoming Territory created and removed from Dakota Territory.

- Laramie City, Wyoming, vigilantes hang Ace and Con Moyer and Big Steve Long for drugging, robbing, and killing their saloon patrons.

1869

- Cheyenne named capital of Wyoming Territory.

- Under the pen name "Ned Buntline," Edward Zane Carroll Judson publishes the first dime novel about Buffalo Bill Cody.

1873

- Multiple factors, including Civil War debt, create the Panic of 1873, beginning a four-year national depression and putting many thousands out of work.

1874

- Custer expedition into the Black Hills helps fuel national belief in "gold in the roots of the grass" there.

1875

- Jenney expedition of geologists assesses the Black Hills, while the government tries to buy them from the Sioux.

- In Custer City, Tom Milligan accidentally kills his friend and mining partner.

1876

- Homestake Mine opens in Lead. Persimmon Bill Chambers and his gang flourish as stage robbers. Madam Mustache opens a brothel in Gayville. "Poet scout" Captain Jack Crawford heads the newly formed Black Hills Rangers.

- January 27—First stage (not a Concord coach) from Cheyenne to Custer City.

- April—Metz family massacre: Stuttering Brown is murdered by robbers. The rush begins from Custer to Deadwood Gulch, emptying Custer City. Hill City, fourteen miles north of Custer City, sees 250 cabins built overnight.

- April 3—First three Concord coaches leave Cheyenne for Custer.

- May 31—Two troops of cavalry and three of infantry are assigned to patrol the Black Hills Trail.

- June—After the Battle of Little Bighorn on June 25, Black Hills Trail traffic nearly stops because of Indian attacks.

- July 4—Cowboy Nat Love claims to have roped, bridled, saddled, and ridden a mustang in nine minutes, winning a $200 purse.

- July 12—Wild Bill Hickok, Charlie Utter, Calamity Jane, and a wagonload of prostitutes arrive in Deadwood.

- July 14—Jack and Jeannette Langrishe's acting troupe brings Shakespeare and melodramas to Deadwood.

- July 16—Buffalo Bill Cody kills and scalps Cheyenne warrior Yellow Hair, in retribution for Custer's death.

- August—Lead, on Gold Run, is founded.

- August 2—Jack McCall kills Wild Bill Hickok.

- August 3—McCall is acquitted of murder at his Deadwood trial.

- August 22—Sam Young kills Bummer Dan (Myer Baum).

- September 25—First through stagecoach arrives at Deadwood from Cheyenne. Deadwood, Whitewood, and neighboring gulches' population is claimed at 10,000 to 12,000.

- November—Performer Banjo Dick Brown kills Ed Shaughnessy from the stage of a variety theater.

- December—Jack McCall is found guilty of murdering Wild Bill Hickok, in a Yankton trial.

1877

- Bill Gay kills Lloyd Forbes. Collins-Bass gang robs at least seven Black Hills Trail stagecoaches. The first Deadwood Dick dime novel is published, with Calamity Jane as a character.

- February—Monroe Salisbury, Jack Gilmer, and Colonel Matt Patrick buy the Cheyenne and Black Hills Stage. Patrick goes to Washington, D.C., to solicit mail contracts, and to Concord, New Hampshire, to order new Abbott and Downing stagecoaches. Boone May kills Curly Grimes.

- February 28—Congress passes bill opening Black Hills to white settlement.

- March 1—Jack McCall hanged in Yankton.

- March 25—Robert McKimie, part of Collins-Bass gang, kills stage driver Johnny Slaughter.

- April—Al Swearingen opens the Gem Theater in Deadwood.

- April 10—First night run of the Cheyenne-to-Deadwood stage.

- June 25, 26, 27—Clark Pelton, Little Reddy McKimie, Dunc Blackburn, James Wall, Bill Bevans, and others rob stagecoaches three nights in a row.

- July—Clark Pelton kills Adolph Cuny.

1877 (CONT.)

- August— Boone May and Prescott Webb shoot it out on Main Street in Deadwood. Vigilantes hang rustler–stage robber Lame Johnny (Cornelius Donahue) after taking him from lawmen.

- October 9—Blackburn and Wall rob both the Cheyenne-bound and Deadwood-bound stages.

- Nov. 23—Scott Davis returns from a solo trek across Wyoming, with Dunc Blackburn and James Wall in custody.

- December 1—Telegraph line completed to Deadwood.

- December 6—Sam Curley kills his wife, Kitty, and himself.

1878

- May—A steel-sided treasure coach nicknamed "Old Ironsides" is proposed for Deadwood to Cheyenne runs.

- June 26—A newcomer stabs Frank Warren for getting him drunk and robbing him.

- July 2—Johnny Brown, Charles Henry Borris, and Charley Ross rob the stage in Whoopup Canyon, wounding three passengers.

- Mid-July—Lurline Monte Verde serves as a nurse for wounded robber Johnny H. Brown.

- August—Frank Towle initiates the ambushing murders of a railroad employee and a deputy sheriff.

- September 13—Frank Towle is killed by Boone May and John Zimmerman while trying to rob a stagecoach.

- September 18—Vigilantes hang rustlers George W. Keating and Orbean Davis in the Spearfish Valley.

- September 26—Clark Pelton, Duck Goodale, and others ambush Monitor treasure coach at Canyon Springs Stage Station; a passenger is killed, and two stageline employees are wounded.

- October 18—Vigilantes take accused Canyon Springs robbers Billy Mansfield and Archie McLaughlin from law officers and hang them.

- mid-December—Boone May decapitates Frank Towle's corpse in order to claim a reward for the outlaw's death.

1879

- Dangerous Dick Davis kills Mother Featherlegs. Madam Bulldog (Sarah Erb) divorces her husband and founds the New Bulldog Ranch. Narrow gauge railroad extends to Deadwood.
- September—Deadwood burns down in a day; rebuilding downtown with brick and stone begins at once.
- December—Singer Inez Sexton arrives in Deadwood and endears herself by refusing to be a prostitute at the Gem Theater

1880

- Irate mother Mrs. Brennan storms Deadwood's schoolhouse, armed, after her son is disciplined for pulling a knife on another boy.
- February 3—Curley Grimes is killed when trying to escape from Boone May and W. H. Llewellyn.
- April—Deadwood paper says the gold rush is pretty much over.
- Summer—Charley Wilson kills Kitty Clide and himself.

1883

- Buffalo Bill Cody obtains a Black Hills stagecoach that becomes part of his show as "the Deadwood stage." Russell Thorp, Sr. purchases the Cheyenne and Black Hills Stage and Company Express.

1884

- February 12—Cowboy Fred Higgins kills prostitute Pearl Leopold in Spearfish.

1885

- Spring—Last stage robbery thwarted by Johnny Owens.

1886

- Standard-gauge railroad reaches Rapid City.

1887

- Harry Longabaugh begins serving eighteen months in Sundance, Wyoming, jail for horse theft, earning his nickname "Sundance Kid."

- February 19—The last stagecoach leaves Cheyenne for the Black Hills.

1889

- South Dakota, North Dakota, and Montana become states.

1890

- Wyoming becomes a state.

1897

- June 28—The Wild Bunch robs a Belle Fourche bank.

- Fannie Hill opens her Lead brothel.

1900

- Dora DuFran opens her Belle Fourche brothel.

1903

- August 1—Calamity Jane dies in Terry, near Deadwood.

1910

- The widowed gambler Poker Alice Tubbs founds her Sturgis brothel.

1980

- Deadwood's last house of prostitution is closed.

CHAPTER ONE

THE MAIN ROAD, A TREASURE COACH & BROTHELS

METROPOLISES AT ROAD'S ENDS
Cheyenne, Deadwood & Lead

The Reverend Joseph W. Cook, the first Episcopalian minister in Cheyenne, had this to say about the city in 1868, when he arrived:

> The activity of the place is surprising, and the wickedness is unimaginable and appalling. This is a great center for gamblers of all shades, and roughs [hoboes] and troops of lewd women, and bullwhackers. Almost every other house is a drinking saloon, gambling house, restaurant or bawdy.

On the previous Fourth of July, the Union Pacific Railroad had created Cheyenne, which promptly became all a terminus town can be. Construction workers blew their paychecks in the abominable fleshpots

Reverend Cook saw everywhere, and generally acted like thirsty, woman-hungry cowboys at the end of long trail drives.

Along with the transient workers, the permanent population blew up to more than 4,000 souls by the time the railroad tracks reached town in November. Cheyenne's nickname soon became the "Magic City," for its quick growth.

The tracks moved on westward, taking the rowdy track-layers with them toward Promontory Point, Utah Territory, where eastward-building crews from California met the westward-building ones in 1869 to link the nation.

When Wyoming Territory was formed in 1868, the Magic City became its capital, and it continued as capital with Wyoming statehood in 1890. Nearby Fort D. A. Russell (today's Warren Air Force Base) supplied soldiers to replace railroad gangs in the saloons, but Cheyenne settled down considerably after the railroad camps moved past—until the Black Hills gold rush, that is.

After the 1874 Custer expedition to the Black Hills reported gold on French Creek, the rush was on. Cheyenne at once became the major outfitting town for prospectors bound for the Hills, but it competed with Yankton, Dakota Territory; Sidney, Nebraska; and Sioux City, Iowa. Prospectors bought gear and supplies in Cheyenne, and either bought stage tickets or waited for a traveling party to organize—for safety from the Sioux Indians. A Chicago reporter who visited Cheyenne in 1875 and Deadwood the following year noted that in the latter town he had recognized "half of the population that I met in Cheyenne last May."

Cheyenne held this prominence until 1886, when the first railroad reached Rapid City, letting people ride the rails directly to the Black Hills. By then, the gold rush was pretty much over anyway.

At the northern end of the Black Hills Trail, Custer City (now Custer, South Dakota) was the Black Hills' first gold-rush settlement, founded in 1875, but it was eclipsed in 1876 by the group of camps that would coalesce into Deadwood: Deadwood, South Deadwood, Engleside, Cleveland, Whoopup, Elizabethtown, Fountain City, and Montana City. Nearby Lead eventually absorbed Central City, Anchor City, Golden Gate, Gayville, South Bend, and Oro.

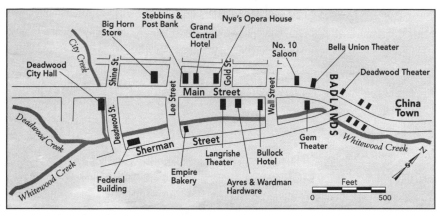

Deadwood in the 1870s.

Deadwood Gulch took its name from a huge amount of downed timber, victim of a wildfire that had passed through. The modern town of Deadwood still faces such a threat from its surrounding forested mountains. It was evacuated inside twenty minutes when a fire moved toward the town in June 2002, then was saved by a fortuitous shift in the winds.

Deadwood briefly reached a peak population of around 10,000 souls in the late 1870s, but numbers declined as easy-to-mine placer gold began to play out. In 1876, crowded deep in Deadwood Gulch, the town was "about three miles long and fifty feet wide," according to stage agent George B. Moulton. Residential streets had to be terraced into the hillsides, with homes built only on one side. Long wooden outdoor staircases connected some of the terraced streets to downtown. During the winter months, direct sunlight in the gulch didn't even begin until noon, and then lasted only three or four hours.

Downtown Deadwood burned to the ground in 1879 and was rebuilt in brick and stone. Only four years later, a major flood floated away many of the low-lying frame or log buildings that had survived the fire.

When the placer gold began playing out in the mid-1880s, Deadwood's population fell dramatically. Many residents—especially those bad boys and wild women—moved on to the next gold strike in search of easy pickings, leaving a quieter and safer Deadwood. (South Dakota's state prohibition of alcohol, passed in 1889 and repealed in 1897, didn't help. Some Deadwood businesses simply shut down.) The remote town and its sister city Lead had direct railroad service only from 1888 until 1930, mainly to carry away the production of the Homestake Mine.

By 1900, half of South Dakota's "manufacturing" wage earners were miners, mostly in Lawrence County—site of both Deadwood and Lead. Statewide, mining, stone quarrying, and well digging employed just over 2,000 wage earners and little more than one hundred salaried staff. Deadwood had become a village rather than a growing town.

It still had plenty of single miners and working men, though, to support the saloons and brothels. National prohibition of alcohol (1919–1933) was openly ignored, and gambling halls flourished until the state government began closing them in 1947. State officials did not close down the final house of prostitution until 1980.

In the 2000 U.S. Census, Deadwood's residents numbered fewer than 1,400. Permitted by state law to make gambling locally legal in 1988, Deadwood literally banks on its Wild West reputation as a resort filled with casinos, modern saloons, and hotels.

Founded in 1876, Lead City (later simply Lead) settled into existence as a more civilized company town whose residents scorned their rowdier Deadwood neighbors. It did have its "tenderloin" district of brothels and saloons, but these enterprises were more discreet than those in Deadwood's raucous "badlands" district on lower Main Street. Lead's tenderloin later disappeared, as the Homestake Mine expanded its Open Cut surface mine from 1918 through 1940.

Lead's city lawmen arrested the town's madams and soiled doves once a month like clockwork, fining them from $5 to $25 apiece. The women probably viewed their fines as something like business licenses.

In Lead (pronounced "leed"), George Hearst's Homestake Mining Company paid salaries that miners and their families could spend in the Hearst Mercantile or Hearst Furniture Store before attending programs at the company-owned Homestake Opera House and Recreational Building. Performance tickets cost money, but the swimming pool, bowling alley, library, and meeting rooms were free of charge. The complex was built in 1914 at the behest of Phoebe Hearst, George's wife. A former schoolteacher, she also had the Homestake Company establish one of the nation's first free public kindergartens for Lead's children.

The Homestake—the largest and deepest gold mine in the Western Hemisphere, but holding low-grade gold veins running through quartz—operated until 2002. Today Lead is an outdoor recreation center, especially during the skiing season.

PAYING BY THE PINCH
Spending & Losing Gold Dust

In the early days, miners carried their gold dust around in small buckskin bags or "pokes." Deadwood's merchants accepted the dust at the value of $18 an ounce, and the proper way to settle a bill was to hand the poke to the merchant or bartender, who used his thumb and forefinger to extract a small pinch of dust and weigh it on his scale.

These men became quite adept at pinching out the correct amount. But they also developed some tricks for their own benefit. The scales sat on small squares of carpeting, not for the decorative touch but rather so that spilled dust could be washed out of the tiny rug at day's end. Bartenders traditionally "brilliantined" (greased) their hair and developed the habit of running their fingers through their locks. When their shifts were over, they washed out the grease and whatever gold dust had stuck to it.

Bartender Sam Young said that he usually got about half an ounce of gold dust, $10 worth, per night.

BLACK HILLS TRAIL
The Deadwood-Cheyenne Road

Most people who rushed to search for Black Hills gold, or to mine its miners, came by way of the stagecoach "road"—such as it was—from Cheyenne. That rough and rutted track remained Deadwood's freight lifeline until the first railroad train reached nearby Rapid City in 1886.

Until then, all the supplies miners needed went into the Hills via freight wagons: blasting powder, tools, guns, clothing, food. In the summer, the wagons carried fresh fruits and vegetables raised in California; during winter, hundred-pound bags of flour, salt pork, and dried beans made up the food offerings—when the wagons could get through the snow.

People traveled the road in Concord stagecoaches, bought rides in and on freight wagons, or even walked beside the wagons to obtain safety in numbers, paying $5 for the privilege.

Beginning in 1876, those with the ready cash could take the relatively quick and comfortable stagecoach. One of these coaches could pack nine passengers inside and six to nine more up on the roof. The interior had three upholstered bench seats; up on top, the "dickey seat" bench was behind the driver and the "China seat" behind it—where the ill-treated "celestials" (from China, which called itself the "Celestial Kingdom") were forced to sit. If need be, two more people could sit on the "boot" with the driver.

A second leather boot hung from the back of the coach, for luggage. Sometimes "shotgun messengers" (armed guards) strapped themselves to this boot—theoretically allowing them to pop around the side and surprise road agents who stood in front of the team to halt the coach.

The driver was assigned to his seat for forty to sixty miles, with the horses changed several times during his ride, both durations depending on weather and terrain. Bad conditions required fresh horses more often—and any stage company worth its salt took good care of its running stock. The driver sat out in the open no matter what the weather, even when snowdrifts between Jenney Stockade Stage Station and Deadwood required putting sleigh-type runners under the wheels. At such times, the drivers dressed in buffalo coats, traded their Stetsons for caps with ear flaps, and wore long, buckskin, gauntlet-style gloves that extended into their coat sleeves—but ice still collected on their beards and mustaches.

At a relay station, horse teams were unhitched, exchanged, and harnessed in about seven minutes. Longer stops at the meal stations allowed passengers to relax from the jolting ride, but Cheyenne-Deadwood travelers rode in the coach from around sixty hours (in good weather) to more than seventy (when weather turned the rutted road to mud). A few "hotels" along the way allowed the more delicate travelers to break up their journeys with an overnight rest of sorts—which often meant nothing better than dozing in a chair.

Frank D. Yates, an Indian trader, and his father-in-law, W. H. Brown, began the first stage line in January 1876, offering service as far as Custer City, via the Red Cloud and Spotted Tail Indian agencies in Nebraska, where they delivered the U.S. mail.

In two months, they sold out to John T. (Jack) Gilmer, Monroe Salisbury, and Mathewson T. Patrick—experienced stage men of Idaho, Utah, and Montana territories. These men owned the line during the Black Hills gold rush heyday. Luke Voorhees, their general manager, also owned a small share; he stayed with the company until 1883 and often participated in posses hunting stage robbers.

In May 1883, these owners in turn sold to Russell Thorp, Sr., who ran the line from his home station at Raw Hide Buttes, in Wyoming Territory between the North Platte and Niobrara rivers. The last coach from Cheyenne to Deadwood left in February 1887.

At first, the stage line extended to Custer City in the Hills, but bigger gold discoveries soon drew miners north of there. Deadwood and its cluster of satellite camps were founded, leading to the search for the perfect route there. Different branches on the northern third of the line were laid out, each touted as the newest and best. One went north from Custer City, one curved east through Rapid City, and another went north on the Wyoming side of the territorial border, then curved south again to reach Deadwood. A mail delivery loop eventually ran from Jenney Stockade to Sundance, Wyoming Territory, then back to Spearfish and Deadwood.

A spur off the Black Hills Trail from Cheyenne ran to Running Water Stage Station (present Lusk, Wyoming, on the Niobrara River) into Nebraska, with a stop at Red Cloud Agency before reaching its terminus at Sidney. Sidney, also on the Union Pacific Railroad, was Cheyenne's lesser competitor for passenger and freight access to the Black Hills.

CONCORD COACHES
New Hampshire's Finest for Deadwood to Cheyenne

What we think of today as the stagecoach of the Old West was the Concord coach. The name came from the town of Concord, New Hampshire, home of the coach manufacturer Abbot, Downing & Company. In the early 1820s, this firm was making the best, strongest, and most comfortable coaches in America. Wells, Fargo & Company used Concord coaches, and so did the Cheyenne and Black Hills Stage Company.

Strong but light hardwoods and fine steel went into these coaches. Every effort was made to keep down the weight, sparing the horses while carrying more passengers. Abbot and Downing's key to success was setting the coach box atop leather thoroughbraces rather than steel springs as their competition did. Mark Twain, who crossed the Plains in one, said it rocked like a baby's cradle rather than bouncing passengers up and down. When it came to day-in, day-out riding, a Concord was a comparatively comfortable way to travel.

Outside, Abbot and Downing coaches were painted a deep, rich red, with bright yellow for the undercarriage. Every coach received elaborate gilt scrollwork, hand-painted by a specialist, as well as landscape paintings that made no two alike.

By the 1870s, many of the Concords in use functioned as does today's hotel limousine, meeting a town's arriving trains to drive patrons from the depot to their lodgings.

THE MONITOR
Deadwood-Cheyenne Treasure Coach

The demand to transport gold bullion out of the Black Hills to the railroad in Cheyenne became apparent by the end of the stage line's first year of operation, in 1876. During the fall, miners were shipping out the fruits of their summer's labors, with one coach heading south filled with $30,000 in gold.

As gold poured out of the Black Hills, the Cheyenne and Black Hills Stage Line increased its security. Regular passenger coaches tried carrying locked, heavy wooden "treasure boxes" under the passenger seats. In 1876 and 1877, robbers shot or dynamited the locks and helped themselves to the gold inside.

The stage line owners then commissioned a Cincinnati manufacturer to send them a special safe called a "salamander," possibly because it was oblong and green. It was iron and lined with steel, sixteen by thirty inches but with walls so thick that its interior storage space was only ten by twenty-four inches. Best of all, it had the newest Yale lock design, which the company guaranteed couldn't be opened for six days after sealing by anyone who didn't know the combination.

At first, the salamander was carried on the line's regular passenger-and-express-mail runs. But that wasn't good enough—it meant that paying passengers traveled with treasure shipments. And passengers weren't happy being put in personal danger that way. So the stage line began separate "treasure coach" runs, on which no passengers were allowed.

After a lengthy series of robberies in 1877, the company ordered what they named the Monitor, an armored treasure coach that cost them $31,000. This was not a modified Concord coach with passenger comforts. It was custom built by A. D. Butler of Cheyenne just to carry gold and shotgun messengers.

In May 1878, when the fortified Monitor went into service, some folks nicknamed it "Old Ironsides." It wasn't made of iron, but the floor and walls were reinforced inside with steel plates more than a quarter-inch thick and could withstand rifle fire. Portholes in the doors supposedly allowed shotgun messengers riding inside to draw a bead on bandits. The salamander was bolted to a steel floor plate. In September that year, the Monitor was joined by a twin named the Johnny Slaughter in honor of a fallen stage driver, but people usually referred to either vehicle as simply the "treasure coach." On its weekly runs, the Monitor carried no passengers except the shotgun messengers, sometimes seated inside, and it often traveled with additional guards as outriders, or with one riding the boot with the driver.

Unfortunately for the Monitor, the competing Deadwood newspapers, the *Black Hills Pioneer* and the *Black Hills Times*, loved to headline stories about how much gold would be on the coach's next run—very handy for the bad boys planning a robbery.

In 1879, the Cheyenne and Black Hills Stage Company began sending the Monitor from the Hills to Sidney, Nebraska, on the Union Pacific Railroad to deliver its treasure. Road agents naturally began moving away from the Black Hills Trail, following their prey.

"RESCUE OF THE DEADWOOD STAGE"
Riproaring Highlight of Buffalo Bill's Wild West
Buffalo Bill Cody started what would become Buffalo Bill's Wild West and Congress of Rough Riders of the World show in 1883, and it toured the United States and Europe through 1915. From the show's creation, one of the long program's highlights came right in the middle of each

This image of a packed Deadwood-to-Cheyenne stagecoach was said to be of its final run. However, the last run occurred in February 1878, and the ground would have been covered in snow, not bare, as seen in this photograph.

performance: an Indian attack on "the Deadwood stagecoach," with rescue by stalwart cowboys.

In fact, Indians hadn't been constant in attacking stagecoaches. Their efforts to drive the whites out of eastern Wyoming and western South Dakota usually focused on stage stations or ranches, where they drove off horse teams or cattle. All the same, Cody had nearly one hundred Indians in his show, and this was one of several acts in which they worked. (Most of the other, lesser Wild West shows portrayed Indians via white performers in makeup and wigs.)

Cody did guarantee authenticity by buying an actual stagecoach from the Cheyenne and Black Hills Stage Company. He contacted manager Luke Voorhees, who supplied a coach for $1,800—a good deal for the stage line because this vehicle hadn't been in use since it had, in fact, been attacked by Indians at Indian Creek. Voorhees told Cody that this particular coach was one that Cody himself had ridden in 1876, when he was near the Black Hills as a cavalry scout.

When Cody and first-year partner Dr. W. F. Carver split up in October 1883, after only one season running the show together, Cody had a good chance of losing the stagecoach. The two decided that the fair way to divide the stock and equipment was to flip a silver dollar, item by item, with the winner having first choice. When the Deadwood coach was up for choosing, the coin toss went Cody's way.

The most unusual showing of the mock attack came during a command performance for Queen Victoria's Jubilee Celebration in 1886. Among her guests were the kings of Belgium, Denmark, Greece, and Saxony—and of course her son, the Prince of Wales and future King Edward VII. Before the mock attack, these five men decided to enjoy the show from inside the coach, and a showman doesn't exactly say no to a king.

When the act was over and the men stepped down, the prince joked to Cody, a fellow poker aficionado, "Colonel, you've never held four kings like these." Cody graciously replied, "I've held four kings, but four kings and the Prince of Wales make a royal flush such as no man has ever held before."

PONY EXPRESSES EVERYWHERE
Riddle of Local Fast-Mail Services

So many obituaries of western pioneers stated that the man rode for "the Pony Express" that today's researcher might wonder who was left at home to write or receive the letters they were carrying. Calamity Jane's "autobiography" claimed that even she rode for the Pony Express.

Solving the riddle means defining "the." Today, when we say "the Pony Express," we mean the fast-mail service that for eighteen months in 1860 and 1861 carried expensive express mail straight through from San Francisco to St. Joseph, Missouri. With mail pouches passed from one tired rider to a fresh one, and horses changed more often at relay stations, the mail made this trip in only twenty-four days.

But there also were small, local fast-mail services all over the West. They too were called "pony expresses." Perhaps Calamity Jane did messenger a letter from one town to another during her lifelong travels. Certainly many men contracted to ride for these services, which were usually run by a stage or freighting company. Some of those fellows survived to get old and tell their grandchildren that they rode pony express, and eventually the tale was proudly passed down in the family that great-grandpa rode for "the Pony Express."

The local pony expresses were, like their national namesake, usually short-lived. Either a camp failed and no longer needed service or the U.S. Post Office arrived to establish regular mail service. Preceding the post office, horseback mail to the Black Hills began in January 1876. People traveling to Cheyenne carried along their friends' outgoing mail, for a fee or voluntarily.

During the summer of 1876, the local Pioneer Pony Express began zipping regularly between Fort Laramie and Deadwood in only forty-eight hours, for just twenty-five cents per letter (in addition to U.S. postage to its destination). At first it ran weekly, but service later was doubled. One of its three partners was "Colorado Charlie" Utter, who had come to the Black Hills with his friend Wild Bill Hickok. Utter was an experienced freighter and arrived planning to offer the Hills both pony couriers and freight service.

But as soon as the Concord coaches began making frequent, scheduled trips on the Black Hills Trail, Utter's pony express shut down.

BROTHELS ALONG THE STAGE ROAD
Hardened & Depraved Wretches
Stage stations quickly became community centers for the few residents in their areas—places to mail a letter or get a drink, enjoy conversation, and, in some, consume a hot meal. Some stations were friendlier than others to local or traveling bad boys.

A few of the stage station "ranches" included low-class brothels, and other brothels stood alone along the route. Such stations included Three Mile and Six Mile near Fort Laramie—aimed at the nearby soldier population. Mother Featherlegs's ranch between Running Water Stage Station and Raw Hide Buttes Station, where the madam was said to assist road agents, was a dive not connected to a stage stop.

Three Mile was opened as a legitimate stage stop in 1873 by Adolph Cuny and Jules Coffey, but the following year it was in financial trouble. The U.S. government was working to get prospectors out of the Black Hills, which were still part of the Sioux reservation, so traffic on the Black Hills Trail had slowed to a trickle. The two businessmen built a few small cabins out back for "cribs," accommodations for prostitutes.

Only the coarsest, ugliest, or most worn-out women worked at the stage stops, and locals called their establishments "hog farms." John G. Bourke, General George Crook's aide, rode out from Fort Laramie one day and later wrote of Three Mile that it was

> tenanted by as hardened and depraved a set of wretches as could be found on the face of the globe...equipped with a rum-mill of the worst kind and...contained from three to half a dozen Cyprians, virgins whose lamps were always burning brightly in expectancy of the upcoming bridegroom, and who lured to destruction the soldiers of the garrison. In all my experience, I have never seen a lower, more beastly set of people of both sexes.

In September 1877, one such denizen, a Mrs. Bloxson who worked at a brothel near the Hat Creek Stage Station, arrived in Deadwood. Wearing men's clothing, she proceeded to get drunk and raise Cain on the main street. The *Black Hills Times* had absolutely no use for her, labeling her "a low down idiotic sort of a prostitute who has been herding with Indians, negroes and soldiers, for the past year."

WYATT EARP
The Spring Cleanup Run
Famed western lawman Wyatt Earp told his biographer, Stuart N. Lake, that he had a brief connection to the Black Hills, when his budding gunslinger reputation helped him serve his employer well.

In the early 1870s, Kansas had a real love-hate relationship with the Texas cattle drovers who brought their cattle to ship from its railroad towns. Shipping points like Abilene and Newton on the Union Pacific Railroad and Dodge City and Wichita on the Santa Fe prospered mightily from the free-spending cowboys' presence at trail's end. The towns built stockyards for the herds and adjusted their annual schedules around these summer visitors. During shipping season, towns added extra lawmen to their otherwise sparse payrolls, and most permanent residents avoided the entertainment districts. And Kansas continued to try to figure out how to enforce its 1868 law banning deadly weapons in the hands of

*Wyatt Earp was about thirty when he posed for a Dodge City, Kansas, tintypist,
around the time of his claimed winter in Deadwood.*

"vagrants, drunks, and former Confederate solders"—a fair description of most Texas cowhands at trail's end.

The cattle drive era lasted for only a decade, but it provided work for Wyatt Earp for four years after he arrived in Wichita in 1875 as a twenty-seven-year-old widower. Once arrested for horse stealing in Indian Territory (modern Oklahoma), he was hired as a policeman in Wichita, then the next year as assistant marshal in Dodge City, where he stayed until 1879.

Winters were quiet times in Dodge City, though, so Wyatt and his brother Morgan went to check out Deadwood in the fall of 1876, between the cattle drive seasons. Morgan didn't like what he saw and quickly left for Dodge to spend the winter. Wyatt thought that his gambling skills at the faro banks and poker tables would see him through nicely. But he later claimed to have supported himself mainly by cutting and selling wood seven days a week.

He also looked around the hills for a likely spot to mine and make some serious money, but he eventually concluded that all the good spots had been staked out by others.

Gilmer, Salisbury, and Patrick's stagecoach was to take out the "spring cleanup" of gold in June 1877, bullion that amounted to $200,000 (worth more than $3.8 million in 2007). They advertised that Wyatt Earp "of Dodge" would be the shotgun messenger and didn't mention that his armaments included a pair of revolvers, a repeating rifle, and a short-barreled shotgun. Earp was probably one of several shotgun messengers, since that trip was only three months after stagecoach driver John Slaughter had been killed, not to mention the fortune in gold aboard.

The stage left Deadwood for Cheyenne right on time at seven in the morning but was only a couple of miles along the way when Earp claimed he noticed horseback riders on both sides of the road, traveling at the same speed as the coach. He shot and killed one of their horses, and that was enough to send all the riders packing.

The spring cleanup reached Cheyenne safely, and Wyatt Earp said he received $50 for his services, good pay for a week's work. He returned to Dodge City for another couple of years before making his way to Tombstone, Arizona Territory. ⇥

CHAPTER TWO

LAW-ABIDING BAD BOYS

GEORGE ARMSTRONG CUSTER
Publicist of "Gold at the Roots of the Grass"

George Armstrong Custer may have done more than any other individual to instigate the Black Hills gold rush, but his one trip there was in the line of duty.

Custer and the U.S. Army were frequently a bad fit, but when his brand of insubordination worked on the battlefield it led to his reputation as the "Boy General" of the Civil War. He had barely made it out of West Point, graduating at the very bottom of the class of 1861, almost losing his chance at a career with improved (for him) social status because he couldn't obey rules and plagued his classmates with practical jokes. He was lucky there was a war going on and the army needed all the trained officers (or semi-trained, in Custer's case) who were available.

Soldiers, Arikara scouts, geologists, reporters, and band members made up the huge Black Hills Expedition led by George A. Custer. This 1874 image is by the Black Hills expedition's official photographer, W. H. Illingworth.
COURTESY NATIONAL ARCHIVES, NWDNS-077-HQ-264-854.

Throughout his fifteen-year career, Custer had detractors and supporters among every rank—right up to the top brass. General Philip H. Sheridan, commander of the Division of the Missouri (one-third of the army, it covered the entire frontier region), was pro-Custer. General William Tecumseh Sherman, commander of the entire show, was just as anti-Custer.

After the Civil War, the army was downsizing, so officers of the middle ranks were facing fewer promotions over their careers and struggling for command positions. Custer's knack for getting personal publicity and standing out in the dwindling crowd led to animosity from others. His frontier field expeditions included journalists whose glowing accounts ran in newspapers across the nation. He frequently wore his blonde hair long and replaced his uniform with frontier-style buckskins and wide-brimmed hats, adding to the romance. The sixteen-piece regimental band added to the crowd, playing the 7th Cavalry's lively jig-tempo theme, "Garry Owen," to announce its departures and arrivals.

When the 7th Cavalry was formed at Fort Riley, Kansas, in 1866, Sheridan wrangled its command for Colonel Custer. Colonel was his real rank, even though he had been breveted a general during the Civil War—a temporary battlefield rank, given as either an honor or a quick promotion after other officers were lost. In Custer's case it was the former, a reward for breaking rules and snatching a military success. And it surely further convinced him that the Custer way of doing things worked well.

To his credit, the colonel was always at the front of his men and shared the hardships of skirmishes, forced marches, and rough trails or weather with never a complaint. Unfortunately, his occasional reckless-ness necessarily included his soldiers. He was also exceptionally good at reading unknown land and choosing the best route for the supply wagons coming behind the cavalry.

Frontier army life was mostly boring. The soldiers drilled and drilled and did chores by day, and most of them drank and gambled by night. A call would come for an Indian skirmish, demanding days of quick, hard riding and fighting, then it was back to the post to kill some more time.

The solution for Custer's favored officers—the young and dashing ones—was to invent social occasions including hunting parties, musicales, theatricals, and masquerade parties. Resentful enlisted men groused that his inner circle was "the royal family." On the post and in the field, Custer surrounded himself with relatives, including brother Captain Tom Custer and brother-in-law Lieutenant James Calhoun. Custer's wife and his sister Margaret Calhoun lived with their husbands on post, perfectly acceptable—although not standard—at the time.

Unusual for the place and time, drinking wasn't part of the Custers' socializing. Tom was known to go on sprees (Wild Bill Hickok arrested Tom in Hays, Kansas, on December 31, 1869, when he shot up the streets before riding his horse into a saloon), but George had become a teetotaler after a youthful indiscretion.

Elizabeth Bacon Custer and her husband George lovingly called each other "Libbie" and "Autie" and acted like the frontier army experience was their perpetual honeymoon. They had no children but owned and pampered a pack of large hunting dogs.

In 1873, the U.S. government had begun trying to purchase the Black Hills from the Sioux nation and to move the Sioux people onto a five-year-old reservation that covered roughly the western half of today's South Dakota, extending into Nebraska and North Dakota. White Dakotans had been agitating that the Black Hills, completely inside the Sioux reservation, be opened for mining. Now that the Northern Pacific Railroad was building west from Bismarck into Sioux lands, aiming for the Yellowstone River in eastern Montana, General Sheridan didn't want the Sioux to have the Hills as a safe place from which they could ride out to raid railroads and settlements.

The army put together an expedition to assess the Black Hills region in 1874, placing Custer at its head. He had already skirmished with the Sioux, including legendary warrior Crazy Horse, when the 7th Cavalry had guarded railroad survey crews on the Yellowstone River. Because Custer had won his few small Indian fights, his take on fighting the Sioux and their Northern Cheyenne allies was that there would be "nothing to it."

From the beginning of July to the end of August 1874, Custer led the Black Hills expedition of a thousand soldiers and a hundred Arikara scouts. President Ulysses Grant's son Fred, a colonel on General Sheridan's staff, went along, as did reporters and the band—and geologists, even though the official purpose was to scout a site for a fort to help control the Sioux. Even though President Grant disliked Custer, the latter thought of the genial Fred as his friend.

Custer treated the trip as a great summer outing, bagging a grizzly bear and climbing (but not summiting) Harney Peak, the Hills' highest mountain. The troops played baseball and toasted winners with nightly champagne parties.

Late in July, panning produced a little gold, and Custer enthusiastically sent scout Lonesome Charley Reynolds out with a dispatch announcing that he had "found gold in the roots of the grass" without working hard at all. Reynolds traveled by night out of Sioux country to Fort Laramie to telegraph the report.

News of easy gold pickings always drew crowds of prospectors, but the timing couldn't have been better for starting a rush. The year before, a deep national economic depression had started, throwing thousands of men out of work. They were an avid audience for news of any job opportunities. The expedition's chief geologist, Newton H. Winchell, pooh-poohed the gold rumors when he got back from the Hills, as did Fred Grant, who thought he might have seen $3 worth of gold during the whole trip. But the word was out, and soon the gold rush into the Black Hills was on.

Fewer than two years later, the Sioux and Northern Cheyenne would take their revenge and wipe out five of the 7th Cavalry's twelve companies at a remote waterway in southeastern Montana Territory, the Little Bighorn. Among the dead would be George and Tom Custer, James Calhoun, and Lonesome Charley Reynolds.

THE EARLIEST MINERS
Sneaking onto the Great Sioux Reservation
Before the early 1870s, very few white men had ventured into the Black Hills, land the Sioux had taken from the Kiowas and considered sacred. Intrepid mountain man Jedediah Smith had crossed the entire Hills in 1823, and in 1833 a party of seven apparently found gold but had been killed by the Sioux before getting out. When Sioux warriors came upon a mixed-blood trapper in 1855, they cut off his hands and cut out his tongue.

Chief Bear's Rib was kinder to Sir George Gore when he met the nobleman's hunting party in 1856, near today's Sundance, Wyoming. Historian Dave Walter labeled Gore, who lived on the income from vast estates in Ireland, as the "first 'slob hunter'" to visit the Upper Missouri River country. Traveling in a caravan of twenty-eight wagons, with servants who loaded his guns for him and guided by Jim Bridger, Gore had just spent two years hunting and fishing in future Wyoming and Montana and claimed to have killed 2,000 bison, 105 bears, and 1,600 elk and deer—collecting only the hides. Indians and their government agents were appalled. As his party was heading down the Missouri to return to Britain, according to historian Jerry Bryant, they met up with Chief Bear's Rib, who took everything they had—including their clothing—and turned them loose. Bear's Rib didn't do as well as he might have, though, because Gore had burned up most of his gear in a fit of pique after a trader at Fort Union, on the Missouri, refused to buy it for what Gore thought it was worth.

Overlapping with Gore's devastation of the animal population, Lieutenant G. K. Warren headed a U.S. Army expedition to explore and map the land north of the Platte River, in future Nebraska, South Dakota, and Wyoming, during 1855, 1856, and 1857. His detailed reports to Congress included the first serious geographical assessment of the region that included the Teton Sioux homeland and the Black Hills. In 1859 and 1860, Captain William F. Raynolds led another military party, which included geologist F. V. Hayden, that explored the northern Black Hills before going on into Montana's Yellowstone River country.

By the late 1860s, rumors of gold persisted, and Wyoming residents weren't the only ones beginning to talk about the treasure hidden in the Black Hills. Before and after Custer's 1874 expedition, more prospectors began sneaking into the Hills.

By doing so, they were breaking federal law, because the 1868 Fort Laramie Treaty had set aside all of today's western South Dakota as part of the Great Sioux Reservation. The government wanted to purchase or lease the Hills for mining; it also wanted the Sioux to settle on their reservation and stop the traditional buffalo hunting that led to conflicts with wagon trains and homesteaders. Army leaders were discussing building forts in the Hills to control the Sioux and keep them on the reservation.

By the time of Custer's expedition, the government was walking a tightrope, trying to accomplish all of these things at once. In 1874, the army warned miners that their wagons would be burned, their gear destroyed, and themselves arrested if found in the Hills. But all the soldiers ever did that year was boot prospectors out and warn them not to return—an order the gold seekers immediately ignored. Six to eight hundred miners were in the Black Hills the next summer.

The two-year-old national depression now combined with a plague of grasshoppers devouring crops in the Midwest led more unemployed men to seek their fortunes.

In 1875, at practically the same time the government was negotiating with prominent Sioux chiefs Spotted Tail and Red Cloud for purchase or lease of the land, a geological expedition escorted by soldiers marched into the Hills. The Sioux concluded that the negotiators were acting in bad faith, not understanding that the purchase proposal was from one branch of government and the exploration from another. It was a recipe for disaster.

That geological expedition was led by William Jenney. The Jenney Stockade, which the party built, was later modified into an important stage station on the Black Hills Trail. Colonel Richard Dodge led the soldiers protecting the scientists. They did their work without being attacked, but the Sioux had been tracking them.

Jenney's report estimated that a "gold field" of about 800 square miles sat under the Black Hills. Widespread newspaper publicity led plenty of the unemployed to gather up what they could and head in, most of them via Cheyenne. Coffers swelled in the Magic City as merchants outfitted miners, rented them hotel rooms, and served them meals.

Also in 1875, President Grant quietly told the army to stop taking action against the miners. Toward the end of the year, he moved control of Indian nations from the Department of the Interior to the U.S. Army and demanded that all the Sioux be on their reservations by the end of January 1876. Some went, but many refused.

When these non-reservation Sioux, along with the Northern Cheyenne and a very few Arikara, whipped George Custer's 7th Cavalry late in June 1876, they were encouraged to evict all whites from their lands. That confidence led to some Indian raids on stagecoaches and freight wagons serving the brand-new communities of Deadwood and Custer City in the Black Hills, as well as to more thefts of horses and mules housed at stage stations along the lifeline Black Hills Trail.

Finally, in 1877, the United States formally purchased the Black Hills in a still-disputed act and officially opened the land to white settlement. By then, Deadwood was already anticipating its first birthday.

JAMES BUTLER "WILD BILL" HICKOK
A Marshal Tried for Murder

He was in Deadwood for only twenty days, but this frontier lawman's gunslinger reputation and his dramatic death in the No. 10 Saloon made the name of James Butler Hickok one of the town's most famous.

Only about ten deaths can be firmly attributed to Hickok's twin revolvers, which he wore tucked into a belt or colorful sash, sans holsters for a quicker draw. Hickok's preferred method of settling a ruckus was a firm voice, backed up by a gun in each hand, talking over a rowdy crowd and announcing, "This has gone far enough."

He worked hard at his shooting skill, practicing daily on targets, but those who witnessed him in friendly competitions claimed that excellent bull's-eye shooting wasn't his greatest strength. On the other hand, some said, no one could beat him when it came to a living target; others claimed that Boone May, the legendary stagecoach shotgun messenger, was even faster as a man-shooter.

Growing up in Illinois, James Hickok was the fourth of six children in the family born between 1830 and 1842. When he was born in 1836, he was the fourth boy, with two little sisters yet to come along. He seems always to have enjoyed solitary pursuits, and he began developing his skill as a marksman at the age of twelve.

His father, William, was a shopkeeper and farmer who took his growing family to Troy Grove, Illinois, the year James was born. William, a religious man, rented space for his shop in a building that was also an Underground Railroad station. He and his sons assisted with the work of transporting escaped slaves northward, on at least one occasion escaping under gunfire with a cart filled with "contraband"—slaves heading for freedom.

After William died in 1852, the older brothers ran the farm and entrusted James with filling the larder with birds and game. Thus he developed his marksmanship with moving targets beginning in his midteens. He also did some freight driving before getting the boring job of leading the mule that marched down towpaths pulling canal boats. After a tremendous fistfight with a supervisor who he said had it in for him, Hickok thought he had killed the man and lit out for Kansas at the age of nineteen.

The young man with Unionist and abolitionist sympathies wandered into the employ of a man connected with the Free-State Army of Kansas. This homegrown militia stood off Missouri "border ruffians" who were attempting to take over Kansas and ensure it joined the Union as a slave state like their own. Being associated with one of the Free-State Army's leaders led to Hickok's first employment as a lawman, when he was elected in Monticello in 1858. He didn't stay long, though. Instead, he spent his last years before the Civil War driving stagecoaches and freight wagons for a major company and seeing the western frontier.

Hickok adopted frontier dress, letting his curly, strawberry blonde hair grow long and favoring buckskin suits (although when staying in town he opted for the stylish, long-coated Prince Albert ensemble). Standing an inch or two above six feet tall, he easily towered over most men of the time. His sad, blue eyes looked out from under straight eyebrows, and a drooping mustache framed his mouth.

Hickok's gunslinger legend began on a July afternoon in 1861 along Rock Creek in Nebraska. He bumped into David Colbert "Colb" McCanles, whom Hickok remembered from earlier days. McCanles was a former lawman who now ran a toll bridge and a pair of ranches, bullied the local people, and traded on his reputation as a former "border ruffian."

The stage company Hickok worked for had installed him as manager of its stage station on land it had bought from McCanles, then failed to pay for. (The company soon would be reorganized by Ben Holladay as the Overland Stage Lines.)

That July day, McCanles took his son, a friend, and an employee to Rock Creek Station to get either payment or the return of the property. He apparently didn't know that Hickok had been assigned there, because he called out for the stage superintendent who had been staying there with his wife. When he saw Hickok, McCanles's greeting was, "What in hell, Hickok, have you got to do with this?"

McCanles entered the station and went back outside, shouting to the superintendent to come and settle the matter, even though the stage line employee had said he had no corporate funds to turn over to McCanles.

Then a shot from inside the building hit McCanles in the heart, killing him instantly. Perhaps McCanles had lifted his rifle and the shooter

Harper's Magazine *presented this image of the Hickok-McCanles fight. It depicts Hickok's version of the tale, which included fisticuffs. Other witnesses said Hickok shot first, from hiding, and killed two men.* NEBRASKA STATE HISTORICAL SOCIETY, COLLECTION #RH2603.

anticipated an attack, but no one knows for sure. While McCanles's son knelt by the body, his friend ran into the building and Hickok wounded him fatally.

The McCanles employee was running away when Hickok set loose a tracking dog, and stage line employees—one carrying McCanles's rifle—found and killed him. The son, who ran from his father's body into the scrub and got away, always claimed that none of the men with him had been armed.

Hickok was arrested, tried, and acquitted of murder. When he told the story in later years, McCanles and his group had turned into a much larger gang of desperadoes that he'd vanquished with his fists and a knife after his ammunition was used up. History buffs have debated for years whether it was cowardly murder or Hickok defending himself and others in the station, including women.

Now that the legend had begun, next came the nickname. Hickok left the area and signed on with the Union army as a civilian scout. One night in Independence, Missouri, he came upon a drunken, angry mob clamoring to lynch a bartender who had shot and wounded one of their number to end a saloon brawl. Hickok faced them down with both guns drawn, fired over their heads, and told them that was enough for one night. It worked. A woman among the bystanders yelled, "Good for you, Wild Bill!" And that was that.

Hickok saw action in the Civil War as a scout and sometime sharpshooter in Arkansas and Missouri and eventually worked as a spy behind rebel lines.

In Springfield, Missouri, a few months after the war ended, Hickok ran into Dave Tutt, a former rebel with whom he may have crossed paths during the fighting. Hickok tried to avoid Tutt's taunting when he was winning at a card game after Tutt had been shut out. Then Tutt picked up Hickok's pocket watch from the card table and announced that he would be walking across the town square carrying it at noon the next day.

Hickok was there at the appointed time and tried to warn off Tutt. But the ex-rebel drew his gun and kept walking. Hickok fired both his pistols and killed Dave Tutt. It took a jury only ten minutes to find him not guilty of murder, but public opinion was divided over Hickok's actions.

Early the next year, Hickok was appointed a deputy U.S. marshal at Fort Riley, Kansas, where uniformed soldiers' morale was low following post–Civil War cuts in their strength just as they were being sent to the frontier to fight Indians. Meanwhile, at Fort Riley, civilian employees like the teamsters and other low-paid workers had for some reason joined ranks against the soldiers. Hickok was able to quiet down the feuding without ever resorting to gunplay. He then turned to a marshal's more mundane duties, like tracking down army deserters.

He was at Fort Riley when the 7th Cavalry was formed there, and Hickok signed on to scout for it, under Colonel George A. Custer, in his spare time. A few years later, Custer gushed in a magazine article that Hickok "was one of the most perfect types of physical manhood I ever saw," whose "deportment...was free from all bluster and bravado. He seldom spoke of himself unless requested to do so. His conversation... never bordered either on the vulgar or blasphemous."

Connections at the fort led to Hickok's scouting for the 10th Cavalry and serving in the 5th Cavalry during the 1868 campaign when another part of the command, Custer's 7th, attacked Black Kettle's Cheyenne camp on the Washita River. After the turn of 1869, Hickok was attacked by some Cheyennes when he was alone, carrying dispatches between commanders. One warrior lanced him in the thigh; he grabbed the lance but, while getting away, ended up losing his horse. Using the lance as a crutch, Hickok continued making his way toward Fort Lyon, his destination, and was finally found by woodcutters working outside the fort at dawn.

As he was recovering, Hickok received word that his mother was seriously ill back home in Illinois, and so he returned there for his first visit in fourteen years. After reaching home, Hickok had to have surgery on the leg wound, which he supposedly did without anesthesia—and while holding the lamp for the doctor to work by. He rested and visited for a few months before heading west again.

In August 1869, Wild Bill Hickok was elected sheriff of Ellis County, Kansas, based at Hays City near Fort Hays. The previous sheriff had been killed in an ambush, and the nearby troops were too busy to answer the town's requests for support. Plains buffalo hunters—generally a rough breed of men—rendezvoused in town, and Union Pacific railroad builders—perhaps a rougher breed—brought their paychecks to Hays's saloons and brothels.

Hickok doffed his buckskins and donned his town clothes, posted notices against carrying guns in Hays City, then turned his diplomatic skills to quieting fights and preventing bloodshed. He had barely assumed the post when one bad guy, Bill Mulvey, drew on him, and Hickok wounded him fatally. The next month, the lawman was challenged again, allegedly over a card game, by Sam Strawhim (or Strawhan). The coroner's jury found that Hickok's killing of this bad boy was self-defense.

After serving his one-year term as sheriff, Hickok left Hays City a much quieter town than he had found it. Unfortunately, when he was visiting there in 1870, five drunken solders from the fort attacked him.

Hickok defended himself and left two dead and one wounded. The good citizens were incensed, and Hickok quickly left town.

As the story goes, on New Year's Eve in 1869, Lieutenant Tom Custer, George's brother, had been drunk and shooting out the Hays street lamps. Hickok and a deputy arrested and jailed him overnight, and Custer paid a fine in court on New Year's Day in 1870. When Hickok returned to visit later in the year, Tom Custer egged on the other soldiers to take revenge for him.

Next to hire Hickok was Abilene, Kansas, suffering from its selection as a shipping point by Texas cattlemen over the previous five years. By 1872 the cowtown had had enough of the rambunctious cowboys and their celebrations after months on the trail, so the city fathers hired Hickok as town marshal, with orders to clean up Abilene. He had the help of three deputies to control crowds of cowhands that could reach 5,000 rollicking souls. As in Hays City, he was replacing a previous marshal who'd been killed, this one by a homesteader he was serving papers on, and again, as in Hays, Hickok posted signs saying no one could wear guns within the city limits.

Because Hickok enjoyed playing poker, he had his favorite saloons. Ever on the alert for a new gunfight challenger, however, he always sat at the card table with his back to the wall, all entrances in view.

He was in Abilene's Novelty saloon on the night of October 5 when a gunshot rang out in the street. Cowhands attending the county fair had been moving drunkenly up and down the street all evening, but now things had gone far enough. Hickok ran toward the sound of the shot.

Phil Coe admitted to being the shooter, claiming his target was a dog. He had previously owned the saloon where he now was house gambler, and he resented Hickok's previous interference with how he'd run that business. As Coe stood with his gun drawn, Hickok pulled both of his on Coe. Just as Hickok and Coe fired at each other, one of the deputies—also drawn by the shot's sound—ran around the building and into the line of fire. Hickok fired again at Coe. The deputy was dead and the gambler dying.

The local paper praised Hickok and his deputies for maintaining order to this point in the cattle drive season and stated that Hickok deeply regretted his deputy's death.

In December, with the season over, the city council released its marshal and his deputies from service—standard procedure. What was not standard was that Abilene's council now declared that the town would no longer serve as a shipping point for cattle drives. The October violence was one factor among several that led townspeople to send cowboys elsewhere.

During 1872, Wild Bill Hickok kicked around for a while, visiting an old Hays City friend, Charlie Utter, at the Colorado boardinghouse he ran, and working as house gambler in a Kansas City saloon. Hickok succumbed to the lures of a show biz income and joined Sidney Barnett's Wild West show touring the area of Niagara Falls, Ontario, and Buffalo, New York. The following year, he joined the show run by William F. Cody and Jack Omohundro, "Buffalo Bill" and "Texas Jack." The three had been friends for a few years and now appeared together onstage, playing themselves in *Scouts of the Plains*, a wild recounting of claimed true-life adventures.

Buffalo Bill was known at the outset of his career as one of the great American showmen, but Hickok took to the stage like a paperweight to water. The voice that could quiet a rowdy saloon crowd came out thin and quavery on the stage, and he was contemptuous of the histrionic deaths around him. He was too much of a loner for the intramural socializing that smoothes the paths of traveling theater companies. He also worried about what effects the spotlights and footlights might have on his all-important vision. Some said he was drinking heavily throughout his time with the show.

Hickok quit in the spring of 1874 and made his way to Cheyenne, then drifted in and out of town that year and the next. He gambled some and also trapped and hunted alone. For the price of drinks, he sometimes spun tall tales for greenhorns, but he turned down would-be challengers with the statement that his shooting days were over, blaming his eyesight. The local sheriff, John Slaughter (not the same man as "Texas John Slaughter"), felt a need to refute in print the rumor that he'd banished Hickok from Cheyenne as a vagrant.

Hickok's excellent biographer, Joseph G. Rosa, speculates that the diminishing eyesight may not have come from age alone, but as a result of gonorrhea. Hickok had had plenty of female companionship over the years, including live-in lovers, and they generally came from the saloon and dance hall arena where he operated. It's certain these women shared the "French disease" (as English speakers once called gonorrhea and its deadlier cousin, syphilis) with many male celebrities of the Old West. Just as certainly, the men's Victorian biographers weren't about to speak of it.

Joseph F. "White Eye" Anderson, twenty-four years old when he traveled to Deadwood in the 1876 Hickok-Utter train, recalled that by then Hickok had no night vision and gladly accepted the younger man's assistance around camp during the dark hours. Others claimed to have seen Hickok wearing tinted glasses in Cheyenne during his last two years there. Historian Rosa searched hard for medical records about Hickok's eye problems but could find none.

In the winter of 1876, Hickok reconnected with an old lover, Agnes Thatcher Lake, who owned a traveling circus. Born either in Ohio in 1832 or in northeastern France in 1826, she was an adventurous woman for her times. She had entered adulthood by running away with a handsome circus performer, Bill Lake, when she was a teenager. At various times she danced, acted in stage plays, tamed lions, and tiptoed across the high wire. The Lakes were touring with their own show at the time Bill Lake was murdered by a disgruntled patron in 1869. The widow kept the circus on the road and was a sharp enough businesswoman to maintain a marginal enterprise.

She met and took up with Hickok in Abilene two years later. Unfortunately, during the relationship, he caught her in the hotel room of another local eligible. After a fistfight, Hickok left Mrs. Lake to his rival. But when he heard, in February 1876, that she was in Cheyenne, he looked her up. Hickok married his older bride (by four or ten years; she admitted to six on the marriage license) early the next month. Their honeymoon was a trip to see her relatives in Ohio, where they visited for two weeks before Hickok returned west alone. He promised, then and in future letters to Agnes, that he'd go to the Black Hills to make a stake for their future and build her a home.

Whether he aimed to make the stake by gambling or prospecting, no one knows.

The Deadwood-bound Hickok-Utter train included old friend Charlie Utter, now going by "Colorado Charlie" in honor of his recent residence; Charlie's brother Steve; the brothers White Eye and Charlie Anderson; and madam Kitty Arnold with a wagonload of prostitutes. At Fort Laramie, a sympathetic military policeman released a hungover and destitute Calamity Jane to the party's custody—provided they would transport her away from his area. Hickok had no use for Jane, and she immediately latched onto Steve Utter anyway.

During the two weeks of travel on the rough road to Deadwood, Hickok practiced target shooting daily—one gun in each hand, and each just as accurate. Sometimes he had White Eye throw his battered old hat up into the air, and he added more holes to it; upon arriving in Deadwood, Hickok would buy White Eye a brand-new hat, at inflated gold camp prices.

Hickok rode ahead on July 11 and selected a campsite on Whitewood Creek, about three miles from Deadwood. The news of the death of old acquaintance George Custer had begun circulating while the group was on the road and greeted them upon their arrival. So did old friends drawn by the area's gold and bright lights. One was Moses E. Milner, the scruffy "California Joe" who had been one of Custer's favorite scouts. He and Hickok spent some time lamenting the cavalry leader's recent death. Given California Joe's great fondness for drink, as well as Hickok's lesser one, they no doubt lifted a glass or a few.

The men began prospecting, which is backbreaking labor for a man of any age. Hickok was now thirty-nine years old. He still wore his hair in long curls, but his wide-brimmed hat hid a hairline that reached nearly to the back of his skull. He'd never held a job for long, and his professional reputation rested on a skill that would fade with age while still attracting deadly challengers.

Such danger came shortly. Hickok heard of six Montanans who were boasting they could take him. He faced them down in a saloon and announced that he hadn't come to Deadwood to gunfight but wasn't averse to causing some funerals rather than taking their insults. This speech he delivered while carefully leaning against the wall. The men backed down, to scornful laughter from the gawking miners.

Hickok's reputation also attracted a job offer from those who wanted to tamp down Deadwood's lawlessness. Would he become the town marshal? Hickok asked for time to think about it. Hays and Abilene had only seasonal bouts with wild cowhands, but Deadwood's bad boys and wild women were year-round residents. Those who didn't leave in the fall would be pretty much stuck here all winter—in close quarters. In both towns Hickok had cleaned up, he had the support of local government, but in the Black Hills there was no government at all. He probably thought, too, about how he could handle trouble that occurred—as so much of it would—during the darkness of long winter nights.

On his twentieth day of camping and prospecting near Deadwood, August 2, 1876, Hickok went into town to play some cards. He hadn't been doing well at the tables, and the more urgent his need to win became, the worse his luck seemed to run. The day before, he had written a short note to his wife: "If such should be we never meet again, while firing my last shot, I will gently breathe the name of my wife—Agnes—and with wishes even for my enemies I will make the plunge and try to swim to the other shore." Hickok couldn't know it, but he'd already fired his last shot.

Dressed in his town clothes, he found a game in progress at his usual table in the No. 10 Saloon, and he asked Charles Rich, who was sitting with his back to the wall, if he instead could take that stool. (The No. 10 had no chairs yet.) With the gambler's superstition that you never give up a "lucky seat," Rich declined. Carl Mann, half-owner of the No. 10, was also in the game—and he teased Hickok that no one would come at him in here. Hickok sat down beside Mann and across the table from Captain William R. Massie, one of the ablest and most famous of the era's steamboat captains. Hickok had beaten Massie at cards the night before.

Hickok could see the front door fine, but he knew there was a small back entrance behind him.

Sam Young was tending bar. Back in Hays City, he'd been in love with a dance hall girl and one night spent all his money entertaining her. Marshal Hickok, watching unobserved, had followed Sam out into the

Arapaho Joe (left) and Charlie Utter at Wild Bill Hickok's first gravesite.
ADAMS MUSEUM AND HOUSE, INC., DEADWOOD, SOUTH DAKOTA.

street and given the younger man good advice about such behavior, then helped him get a government freighting job. When Hickok first walked into the No. 10 not three weeks earlier, Sam had greeted his old friend enthusiastically.

Colorado Charlie Utter came in and started to watch the game, but he didn't join in and soon went back to his and Hickok's shared camp.

A few hands had been played, and Massie was beating Hickok when a drunken Jack McCall came in the front door. The card players ignored him. He went over to the bar and sidled down it—then sprang behind Hickok's back and fired his gun, shouting, "Take that!"

Across the table, Captain Massie felt his own left wrist go numb, and he looked up in confusion. Some say he ran out into the street shouting that Hickok had just shot him for winning.

Hickok, his head down, was still for a moment and then crumpled to the floor, dead. According to Rosa's definitive biography, the hand of cards he dropped was the ace and eight of clubs, the ace and eight of spades, and either the jack or queen of diamonds (debate continues about this fifth card)—and poker players still call a hand with those two black pairs the "dead man's hand."

McCall backed out the rear door and didn't get far before he was captured.

All the card players had run out the front door shouting, starting the news down the street, then went back inside the No. 10 and locked the doors. They designated themselves a coroner's jury on the spot and determined that the bullet had gone through the base of Hickok's brain and out the right cheek. It lodged in Captain Massie's left wrist, where he would carry it until his own death in 1910.

Wild Bill Hickok was buried at his Engleside prospecting camp the next day, but three years later, Colorado Charlie had the body moved to Deadwood's new Mount Moriah Cemetery. In the interim, the widow Hickok came to view the original grave in September 1877. She announced that, once Deadwood's permanent cemetery site was decided, she would fund a "fenced monument to his memory." Then she and her escort, George Carson, took the coach to Cheyenne, where they were married before the month's end.

Hickok had lived as a law-and-order man who broke the law when he saw fit. Many times, over the years, he had warned young men off gambling at cards, and, in the end, he should have taken his own advice.

SAMUEL FIELDS
"General" with a Gift of Gab

Born a free black man in Louisiana, Samuel Fields was about twenty-seven when he arrived in Deadwood in 1876, and he promptly became a local character. Having served in the Union army as a youthful infantry private during the Civil War, he now promoted himself to general. He seemed to seek the limelight, and soon the newspaper was covering his pronouncements and doings, calling him "General Darky" and other even more offensive terms commonly used at the time.

Fields began working as a waiter and porter for the International and other hotels in Deadwood. Like many other hotel employees, he was known to locate female companionship at the request of guests and was willing to deliver other very private communications. Answering the questionnaire for the 1878 city directory, he gave his occupation as "cosmopolite."

Unfortunately for Fields, two years later Mrs. Minnie Callison— Deadwood's first public school teacher—was murdered. Some residents said they had seen Fields near her home that evening, and bootprints matched Fields's size. Minnie's husband, John Callison, was convinced that Fields had done the deed, and Fields was arrested for questioning, though he was later released.

Historian Jerry Bryant states that few people agreed with John, but rather believed that a man named Martin Couk killed the teacher, because she had somehow learned that he was planning to run off with another man's wife.

A few months later, the "General" somewhat redeemed himself by preventing a woman named Annie Simms from killing herself. But some folks always thought he got away with murder in the case of Mrs. Callison.

Remembered as a gifted public speaker on street corners around town, Fields was subjected to heckling by crowds who considered this an entertaining pastime.

Fields later moved to Omaha for a year, returned to work at a Rapid City hotel in 1890, then disappeared from history.

JOHN B. "JOHNNY" OWENS
Brothel Manager, Gambler & Honest Sheriff

Johnny Owens won the Chug Springs Stage Station in an 1870s poker game, old-time freighter Dub Meek claimed. Owens was a professional gambler, a mean hand with a six-shooter, but was also one of the most respected men in Wyoming Territory. And then he became the sheriff of Weston County, elected for fourteen years beginning in 1892.

He was honest to a fault, didn't smoke or drink, and kept his handsome face and slim body well groomed and dapperly dressed. Both the law-abiding and the outlaw respected Johnny Owens for his straightforwardness. You knew where you stood with Johnny, a quiet, well-mannered, friendly man.

Since 1871, Owens had managed the whorehouse at Three Mile Stage Station (three miles from Fort Laramie, that is), one of the route's "hog ranches," homes to low-class prostitutes.

He later ran Chug Springs Stage Station, 200 miles down the road from Deadwood, until 1876, when the stage line moved its stop from the springs to John Hunton's Bordeaux Ranch. One of Owens's problems at Chug Springs was Sioux raiders running off the stage company's livestock during the Great Sioux War.

Owens was an excellent marksman. In Cheyenne in 1876, he joined the rarified ranks of those who participated in a shooting match with Wild Bill Hickok. Like Hickok, Owens was said never to have to stop and take aim. And he beat Hickok in target shooting with rifles—one of several men who could.

Johnny Owens thwarted the very last attempt to rob the Deadwood-Cheyenne stagecoach, in 1885. Outlaws cavorting at the Three Mile hog ranch mentioned their plans in passing, not knowing or caring that Owens considered the stage line's then owner, Russell B. Thorp, Sr., a friend to whom favors were owed. So Owens took off and galloped his horse south to Chug Springs, arriving in time to catch the stage waiting while the horses were changed.

George Lathrop, one of the stage line's best drivers, was on the boot that day. He had a soldier as escort, because Fort Laramie's payroll was on board. Owens told Lathrop to convince the soldier to ride inside so that he himself could sit on the boot, his rifle across his lap and his twin six-shooters in his belt. Only a few miles up the road, three road agents appeared with the greeting, "Halt! Throw up your hands." Owens waited a moment, then waved his hand, answering "Not tonight, boys." The bad boys decided not to try their luck against the gunslinger and disappeared.

Owens opened a saloon and dance hall in Lusk, Wyoming Territory, when the railroad arrived in 1886, but only three years later he packed up and moved north to Newcastle in Weston County, on the west side of the Black Hills. There he opened the House of Blazes, a saloon whose name, locals believe, came from the number of times guns blazed inside its walls.

In 1892, Owens was elected Weston County sheriff and served for fourteen years. He is credited with ridding the area of cattle rustlers, killing twenty men along the way—but always in self-defense.

SCOTT "QUICK SHOT" DAVIS
Captain of the Shotgun Messengers

Short and stocky, Walter Scott Davis left home in Nebraska when he was fifteen and headed west. He was twenty-four when he joined a railroad construction crew in 1868. In 1876 he landed in Cheyenne and was hired by the Cheyenne and Black Hills Stage Company as a freight wagon driver. That was his job in the early months of 1876, when the Sioux frequently attacked travelers on the Deadwood road, still hoping to drive whites out of the Black Hills.

Davis was driving a twenty-mule-team wagon toward the Hills that year when he and freighters for three other companies were attacked at Indian Creek, near the Hat Creek Stage Station. They pulled their wagons together for defense and held off the Indians for three hours. Luckily, before they ran out of ammunition, Captain James Egan's cavalry troop arrived from Raw Hide Buttes. General George Crook had recently assigned this elite company to patrol the Cheyenne road. Even though fourteen head of livestock were killed or injured, only one of the freighters was even wounded.

The following year, Davis became head of the stage line's shotgun messengers, who always accompanied the treasure coach. He usually rode on the boot with the driver. Depending on the size of the gold shipment and recent robbery activities, one or more other shotgun messengers rode on the boot, inside the coach, or strapped onto the back boot.

Even a large number of armed escorts didn't stop some robbers. On September 26, 1876, Davis was with John Denny on the treasure coach's rear boot, and Alex Benham, a stock tender and northern division agent, sat with the driver. At Jenney Stockade, the coach added some soldiers riding inside. And still the coach was stopped—by robbers who turned out to be Dunc Blackburn and James Wall.

Scott Davis was shot in the right thigh during the altercation. A month later, he was able to walk with a cane. In November, he was back at work.

Davis's extreme devotion to the stage line is revealed in the excruciating 375-mile trek he took that November, after Blackburn and Wall stole eight of the company's fine horses from the Lance Creek Stage Station. With manager Luke Voorhees's permission, Davis took five soldiers from Fort Laramie and found the horses' trail, crossing Wyoming to the Sweetwater River valley in heavy snow. There the soldiers dropped out, claiming their horses were spent, but Davis went on alone. When his own horse gave out, he simply traded it at a ranch—without asking permission.

Davis crossed the crest of the Rockies at South Pass and on a hunch took a southbound stagecoach to the Alkali Stage Station, arriving at night. There he discovered Blackburn and Wall, and within twenty-four hours captured them. (This story is told in Chapter Four.)

When Davis arrived back at Cheyenne's train station on November 23, he was amazed to see a big crowd, which included his boss, Voorhees. Davis asked Voorhees what was going on. "They came down to get a look at a man who had nerve enough to capture two road agents," came the answer.

For all his loyal service, Davis falls into the good bad boys category because he seems to have gone too far. After the Canyon Springs robbery in 1878, he led one of the posses searching for the road agents. Two men hanged near the Jenney Stockade were commonly believed to have been found by Davis's group, who took that vigilante action. Whether the hanged men actually participated in that particular robbery is not known.

Davis later satisfied his need for adventure as a special guard for the Union Pacific Railroad, then eventually slowed down enough to work as its livestock inspector for three decades. He died in 1927, in Denver.

VIGILANTES
Taking Law Enforcement into Their Own Hands
Old West mining-rush communities had a tendency to spring up far from established law officers and courts. The territorial capital was often days away by horseback, and no telegraph lines had been built yet. Raw

little mining camps were totally isolated kingdoms unto themselves. In the case of the Black Hills gold rush, Sioux warriors trying to drive out the whites made cross-country travel even more dangerous. This lack of organized law, combined with the wealth of newfound gold, made Custer City, Deadwood, Gayville, and the others extremely attractive to bad boys and wild women.

The chance for financial and political new beginnings attracted law-abiding sorts as well as those of the other persuasion. When the former had had enough of the bad boys, some of these men organized "vigilance committees." Usually short-lived, such groups drew up rules and secret membership lists and passwords, went out and caught the murderers and robbers, maybe gave them brief trials on the spot, and sentenced them either to hanging or banishment ("Get out of town by sundown."). Sentences were executed at once; there were no appeals.

Vigilantes weren't a major force in the Hills, but a few committees do pop up in the records. Sam Young tells about the Custer City Scouts, which organized in 1875 in his own saloon. Its purpose was not to do any scouting but rather to protect woodcutters from Sioux raiding parties, because the small groups cutting the timber needed to build Custer City were attacked often. After two men were killed, the Scouts came into being. Five men were appointed to guard the lumberjacks, with Captain Jack Crawford (at his own request) named the head Scout.

In June 1877, horse thieves A. J. Allen, Louis Curry, and James Hall were captured and jailed in Rapid City. The next night a mob broke into the jail and hanged the three men. After leaving the bodies on display for a few days, the unknown group buried them and placed a warning sign on the grave, no doubt trying to show it was a group of vigilantes rather than just an angry mob. The sign even presented its dire message in verse:

Horse Thieves Beware
Here lies the body of Allen, Curry and Hall.
Like other thieves they had their rise, decline and fall;
On yon pine tree they hung till dead,
And here they found a lonely bed.
Then be a little cautious how you gobble horses up,

For every horse you pick up here, adds sorrow to your cup;
We're bound to stop this business, or hang you to a man,
For we've hemp and hands enough in town
to swing the whole damn clan.

Lame Johnny (Cornelius Donahue) was done in by a gang of eight vigilantes in 1879 on the Deadwood-Sidney road after a three-year career of horse thieving and highway robbery.

Cheyenne, on the other end of the Black Hills Trail, had sported a vigilance committee in January 1868, when it was a young railroad terminus. These vigilantes' first act was non-fatal. When three men were bailed out of jail while awaiting trial for robbery, the vigilantes captured them, shook them down, tied them together, and released them wearing a sign:

> *$900 stole...$500 recovered...Next case goes up a tree.*
> *Beware of the Vigilance Committee.*

The committee wasn't as nice later that month, riding thirty miles west to Dale City to hang three bad boys they'd just kicked out of Cheyenne. At the end of January, the Cheyenne city government was organized, so there was no longer need for the vigilantes. Still, only two months later, the vigilantes returned for a final act.

Charles Martin and Andy Harris had established their Keystone Dance Hall, it was believed, with money they "earned" via strong-armed robbery. Both had records of being very willing to shoot at their fellow man, and Martin especially wasted his time in gambling and drinking. After Martin shot and killed Harris, a jury acquitted him. He was celebrating in the Keystone when four or five masked men broke in and grabbed him. As they took him outside, they fired at the Keystone's door to keep the other patrons—including a city policeman—inside. Then they hanged Martin in the street.

Being on a roll that night, these vigilantes went on to the Elephant Corral, a freight depot and stock corral near the railroad tracks. There they found and hanged Charles Morgan, who was awaiting trial on the charge of mule theft. Many law-abiding residents seemed to think the vigilantes were fighting the good and necessary fight, because they had expected Morgan to be acquitted in court.

One midnight two weeks later, however, an established local brewer who owed a pot of money to a Cheyenne saloonkeeper opened his door to a group of men, who killed him. Local opinion turned against the vigilantes, with people fearing that the saloon owner might have commandeered the committee for his own purposes. After losing public support over this death, Cheyenne's vigilantes closed up shop permanently. ⊹⊷

CHAPTER THREE

KILLERS INTENTIONAL & NOT

TOM MILLIGAN
"He's My Best Friend!"

In his autobiography, Sam Young tells the story of what he believes was the first killing of a white man "by one of his own race in the Black Hills." Young is best known as the bartender on duty at the No. 10 Saloon when Jack McCall killed Wild Bill Hickok.

This supposed "first" took place in 1875, in Custer City. Young, co-owner of a saloon there, had recently (and reluctantly) been appointed deputy town marshal.

He was at a barbershop and had just gotten his face lathered for a shave when gunshots rang out in the street. Young ran out to see what the trouble was, wiping foam from his face. He found a crowd gathered around Tom Milligan, whom they had disarmed just after he fatally shot his partner, Alex Shaw. Young and two other men rushed the man into a nearby cabin and barred the door to protect him.

Milligan slumped to the floor, crying, and blurted, "My God, is he dead? He is my partner and the best friend I ever had in the world." (Or, it's useful to say, that's how Milligan's anguished but eloquent statement ended up in Young's published autobiography.) The story was that Milligan and Shaw had been drinking and were so intoxicated when they left the saloon that they "staggered out." The partner suggested that Milligan shoot an oak bucket at a public well down the street, which seemed like a good idea to Milligan, so he did it.

Then Shaw requested a replay—which Milligan thought was a great idea—but just as Milligan fired the second time, the drunken Shaw lurched in front of the gun and took Milligan's bullet in the head.

By the time Deputy Young got the story put together, others had joined the crowd—mostly men who hadn't witnessed the accident—and were starting to talk about lynching Milligan. Young faced them down and said he was going to guarantee that Milligan got a fair trial the next day. He convinced only part of the crowd to give up on a quick hanging and so sent a friend to his saloon to pick up a shotgun and a rifle. Young was determined to protect Milligan all night.

Several friends offered to help, but Young told them they could do more good by mingling with the crowd and persuading folks not to do anything rash. Then he spirited Milligan off to Young's own cabin, gave him his choice of guns, and stayed on watch with him until nine the next morning. Through this whole time, no one could find Custer City marshal John Burrows.

In the morning, when the pair arrived at Custer City's temporary courtroom, a large crowd was gathered. Burrows was present and being "very officious" as he organized the trial. In short order, the jury acquitted Milligan of murder but fined him $25 for firing a gun in town. Then all—including the grieving Milligan—went off to bury the dead partner.

Not everyone was pleased with the jury's verdict. Sam Young told Milligan he should leave Custer City for safety's sake and lent him his own horse for transportation. Milligan was gone by ten that evening and handed over the horse to Ed Young, Sam's brother, when he arrived at Fort Laramie.

Sam Young never knew what happened to Tom Milligan after that, but he himself "did not want any more of the 'marshal business' and resigned the following day."

WILLIAM F. "PERSIMMON BILL" CHAMBERS
Murderous Horse Thief & Road Agent

How Bill Chambers came by the moniker "Persimmon," no one knows. He claimed to prefer the nickname "Government William," he once told a group of men, because the U.S. government was among his most frequent victims. His audience, met on the trail, was terrified when Chambers identified himself, but this time he was sober and in a mood for talking rather than doing evil. They all camped together and the bad boy gave his autobiography. No one knows how much of it is true, as historian Doug Engebretson wrote when he recorded the story.

Chambers stole and sold horses and guns, robbed stagecoaches and freighters' and pilgrims' camps, and was all too willing to shoot his victims in the process. When shooting, he was accurate with both revolver and rifle, and he could fan the revolver's hammer rapidly. Chambers, of average height and appearance, was said to be so good at disguises that no one recognized him when he so desired. He was also pretty handy at escaping and never went to trial.

Raised in the Appalachian Mountains of North Carolina, not far from the Georgia border, Chambers said he joined the Confederate army during the Civil War. Captured by Yankees, he joined their army—a choice offered some soldiers who might prefer service over prison camp; they then were called "galvanized Yankees." After shooting a fellow soldier in a fight over a woman, Chambers deserted and rejoined the Rebs until he was captured again and sent to a Union prison camp for the war's duration.

By the time he arrived in Cheyenne in 1867, Chambers was in his early twenties and had developed a weakness for whiskey consumed during serious sprees. This penchant led to his meeting a certain class of people, the kind who made their livings by robbery.

The brand-new town of Cheyenne was at this time the rough terminus of the Union Pacific's westward-building section. Chambers and some of his friends fell into the hands of Cheyenne vigilantes, who hanged a couple of the robbers but let Chambers go if he promised to leave town. It wouldn't be the first time he apparently was able to talk himself out of trouble.

He drifted around, next getting into trouble in 1870 at Sioux City, Iowa, on the Missouri River. The whiskey did it again. Drunk and rampaging up and down the streets, Chambers shot his own horse. Deputy Sheriff John McDonald, wanting to prevent injury to a citizen, arrested Chambers—and was shot in the arm in the process.

Chambers somehow escaped from jail, though still manacled. Then he returned to drinking. Soon enough, Sheriff McDonald found and rearrested him. Chambers suggested that the manacles be removed, and the sheriff naively obliged. On a stolen horse, Chambers promptly left Sioux City behind him. The town began offering a $1,000 reward for him, but it never would be collected.

Returning to Wyoming, he became a horse and weapons thief. When the Black Hills stagecoach began service in 1876, Chambers added "road agent" to his resume. He claimed never to rob "poor men" or women— unless the latter were transporting gold on behalf of an obviously rich man.

As a horse thief, Chambers organized a gang that stole horses from cavalry outposts and also from his sometime allies on the Great Sioux Reservation—from the Black Hills to Colorado, he said. According to Agnes Wright Spring, the gang hung out mostly near where the Deadwood road crossed the Cheyenne River, where coaches had to slow down to thread their way down the banks. Chambers was friendly with the reservation's residents, and they never gave him away. In 1875, federal agents put this bad boy before a grand jury, but he once again talked his way out of trouble.

The following year, when most of Fort Fetterman's troops had moved north as part of General George Crook's command in the Great Sioux War, Chambers boldly visited the fort's sutler store. He genially asked some officers to "take a drink" with him, and they refused. Some enlisted men also turned him down. Chambers drew his gun on the unarmed soldiers, loudly identifying himself, and grabbed a bottle of whiskey and some cigars before leaving. On the road he passed a lone soldier, then remembered he had recently seen this man displaying a wad of money at Chug Springs Stage Station on the Black Hills Trail. Chambers shot the sergeant in the back and took his watch and money. Soon a federal reward offered $1,000 for Persimmon Bill. When he heard of a man in Deadwood who wanted to earn that reward, Chambers said he would go there and "take care of him."

Given Chambers' evil side and his friendship with the Sioux, it's no surprise that people suspected him of staging the Metz family massacre around this time and killing Stuttering Brown (see below). After those events, Chambers disappeared from the Black Hills area. Some say either Boone May or Chambers' own gang killed him, but others claim he took his money home to North Carolina and put his criminal past behind him—and still others say he went to Tennessee, where he was hanged.

H. E. "STUTTERING" BROWN
Killed by Persimmon Bill?

H. E. Brown had a severe stutter, but that didn't stop him from being an astute businessman and horse trader. He had been a stagecoach driver and then a stage company manager in Salt Lake City. At the beginning of 1876, he was a supply contractor for southeastern Wyoming railroad construction camps. When veteran stage line owners Jack Gilmer, Monroe Salisbury, and Mathewson Patrick decided to begin Black Hills operations early that year, they hired Brown to be their stage line manager.

As their agent, Brown bought the existing line from Yates and Company in mid-February, then announced good news for Black Hills residents: Beginning on March 1, the new Cheyenne and Black Hills Stage Company would run daily coaches between Cheyenne and Custer City (Deadwood would shortly boom and become the terminus). Yates and Company had run only twice a week.

Made manager of the stage road's northern division (north of Fort Laramie), Brown stocked the new company's stage stations with excellent horses. He was pleased to report progress to the line's general manager, Luke Voorhees, in Cheyenne. But purchasing that fine horseflesh soon brought Brown up against "Persimmon Bill" Chambers, the horse thief based in the Cheyenne River–Hat Creek section. Instant dislike was mutual between the two men, who had such different plans for the new horses. To top it off, Chambers and his men began robbing stagecoaches and freight wagons as soon as these began traveling the Black Hills Trail.

Then came the night in mid-April when Stuttering Brown, stage line employee Charlie Edwards, and driver Silvin Bishop "Curly" Ayres were traveling south from Custer City in a fast-freight wagon, leading a small herd of mules. Stopping at Lew Hagers's ranch at the Cheyenne River, Brown learned that a stagecoach team he'd placed there had been stolen.

Apparently Chambers was also at the ranch, and Brown said he'd kill the horse thief if he didn't move his work elsewhere. Chambers muttered that he'd see about that and then took off.

Brown's party was expected at the Hat Creek Stage Station that night, but the men were nearly twenty miles north of it when gunfire rang out and bullets pinged into the wagon, one finding its mark in Brown. The terrified team in harness ran off, leaving only the mules.

Brown told the other two men that he was wounded too badly to travel and that they should save themselves. Edwards and Ayres helped him mount a mule anyway, and they rode off, hoping to get him aid in time.

When Brown's party didn't show up at Hat Creek as expected, men from that station started north to find it. They found Brown lying on the ground beside the waiting mule. The agent kept asking to speak to Luke Voorhees before he died.

Someone from Hat Creek rode south to Fort Laramie and sent a telegraph to Voorhees in Cheyenne. Voorhees instantly telegraphed back to Fort Laramie, requesting army help for the popular agent, and a wagon carrying the fort's assistant surgeon set out for Hat Creek.

Starting from Cheyenne, Voorhees was well behind them. He rode horseback, changing steeds at stage stations every ten miles, and passed Fort Laramie after nine grueling hours in the saddle. He still had half again that far to travel to reach Hat Creek.

But before he arrived there, Voorhees met the surgeon's wagon coming south, carrying Brown's dead body. Stuttering Brown had lived about twenty-four hours after the shooting, never saying anything but that he had to tell Voorhees something.

At first people blamed area Indians, because earlier in April the Charles Metz family had been massacred in Red Canyon. They had closed down their bakery in Custer City and were on their way home to Laramie with the profits. Their bodies were filled with arrows, then scalped and mutilated.

Some area residents, though, suspected Chambers. Indians almost never attacked at night, they said, and maybe Chambers had even set up the Metz massacre to put the blame on Indians for his own evil deed. The question was never resolved, but those who knew of Brown's confrontation with Chambers the very night he was attacked felt sure they knew who the killer was.

Cheyenne mourned the loss of Stuttering Brown. Business leaders there felt beholden for his hard work at getting a good stage service running. Brown's wife and son traveled to Cheyenne to claim his body, and stage line owner Mathewson Patrick escorted them back to Omaha for a second funeral.

In the long run, Brown's death led to added protection for the stage line. Wyoming's territorial governor, John Thayer, appealed to General George Crook for a greater military presence on the road. As a result, Crook assigned cavalry troops under "Teddy" Egan to patrol especially the Red Canyon–Hat Creek section of the stage road. Brown would have been pleased.

JACK McCALL
Mysterious, Cowardly Shooter of Wild Bill

When he arrived in Deadwood in the spring of 1876, John (Jack) McCall was calling himself Bill Sutherland. He was a twenty-five-year-old Kentuckian who said he had driven stagecoaches, and he might then have started working as a freight driver. He stood about five feet six inches tall; he had chestnut hair that fell over a low forehead, full lips, a thin mustache, and crossed eyes.

Wild Bill Hickok was playing cards at the No. 10 Saloon on the night of August 1, seated as always with his back to the wall, and was way up on the other players, who included riverboat captain William Massie.

When a player left, "Bill Sutherland" took his place. He too lost to Hickok and ended up broke. Hickok gave him enough money to get a meal.

The next day, McCall found Hickok at the card table again, with Massie, saloon co-owner Carl Mann, and others, but this time without having his back protected. McCall shot Hickok from behind before Wild Bill even knew he was there. Hickok fell dead.

Immediately after killing Hickok, McCall pointed his gun at Mann and challenged him and the other men sitting stunned around the card table: "Come on, ya sons of bitches!" His gun misfired as he pulled the trigger on bartender Sam Young and then George Shingle, who was standing at the bar. Covering himself, McCall then backed out the rear entrance.

Hickok's companions locked the saloon's doors after yelling the news out into the street.

McCall tried to steal a horse tied in back of the No. 10, but its owner had loosened the saddle because the day was so hot, and McCall ended up on the ground. Trying to run for it, he was soon captured by an excited crowd.

Deadwood's business owners—the closest thing to a government—took over James McDaniels's Deadwood Theatre for the trial the next morning. Judge W. L. Kuykendall presided over what was, in effect, a miners court—one of the unofficial venues for settling mining-claim questions—and he appointed a prosecutor and a defense attorney. Twelve miners, their names drawn from an almost exhausted supply in a hat, were named to the jury after swearing they hadn't formed an opinion about the crime. The theater was filled with men, each of them (except the prisoner) armed.

When given the chance to speak, McCall said loudly that Hickok had killed his brother. "Wild Bill threatened to kill me if I crossed his path. I am not sorry for what I have done. I would do the same thing over again."

His defense attorney claimed that Hickok was known to kill men for no good reason.

At nine o'clock that evening, the jury returned a not-guilty verdict. (Research by author-actor Thadd Turner shows that the Deadwood Theatre hosted a performance that night, and so Kuykendall had moved the proceedings back to the No. 10 Saloon for their conclusion.) McCall's friends cheered while Hickok's roared their anger and charged that the jury had been bought. Hickok's pal Colorado Charlie Utter vowed vengeance.

Amazingly, McCall didn't leave Deadwood right away. A few days later, California Joe (Moses Milner) went to McCall's cabin and hailed him. Joe had been away checking rumors of a strike at Crook City when his old friend Hickok was killed, and he now informed McCall that the climate here no longer agreed with him. Then he stood and watched as McCall walked out of town.

The killer made his way to Laramie, Wyoming, where he told the newspaper that he recognized Wild Bill from Hays City, Kansas, and that Hickok had shot McCall's brother. McCall made other unsupported claims: Hickok had "as good as robbed" him in a poker game the day before his death, they had argued, and McCall had slapped Hickok's face but got only laughter in return.

On that August 2, McCall said, he had warned Hickok before shooting, received only a smile, then fired. But on another occasion, when a reporter asked McCall why he shot Hickok in the back, the killer answered, "I didn't want to commit suicide."

McCall said he had three mining claims at Deadwood and planned to return there for the winter.

Legal minds in Dakota Territory went to work and concluded that McCall's Deadwood trial was invalid because it was held outside a legitimate court's jurisdiction: Deadwood's site trespassed on the Sioux reservation until the following year, so the town could not have a legally organized government. Therefore, McCall had never been tried, and double jeopardy didn't pertain. He was arrested in October, with a new trial date set for late in November. (Calamity Jane would falsely brag that she not only captured McCall in Deadwood but also was responsible for obtaining the second trial.)

McCall was jailed in Yankton along with another murderer. The two joined forces to beat up the jailer early in November, but they walked out the front door just as the marshal and his assistant were approaching. End of escape.

The trial opened with the court informing McCall that witnesses he requested couldn't be found, then it turned down his request for a postponement until spring. He proceeded to cuss out the judge.

Only prosecution witnesses testified: Carl Mann, George Shingle, and Captain William Massie. Shingle, who had known Hickok for ten years, said he watched McCall enter the saloon and quickly move behind Hickok to fire while the others were focused on their card game.

The killer did not speak during this trial, and his lawyer's only defensive efforts were attempts at legal maneuvers—all of which the judge rejected.

McCall was pronounced guilty on December 6, and a month later he was condemned to hang, on March 1, 1877. The execution went off on schedule and smoothly, McCall attended by a priest and asking for a moment to pray before the drop.

HARRY "SAM" YOUNG
A Fatal Case of Mistaken Identity
Three weeks after Wild Bill Hickok's death, the No. 10 Saloon was the scene of another fatal shooting, this time by bartender Sam Young.

It seems that Young had a beef going on with Laughing Sam Hartman, who gambled at the No. 10 and other saloons when he wasn't out robbing stagecoaches. Some say the point of contention was a woman, but no one knows. Even though Young later wrote an autobiography (hailed more for its color than its trustworthiness), he totally left out the story of this shooting. The tale is to be found in historian James McLaird's detailed introduction to an edition of Young's autobiography.

Hartman had publicly threatened to kill Young, once even standing in the No. 10 and asking co-owner Carl Mann for the loan of a gun to get the job done right then and there. Subsequently, Young was on edge all the time.

Hartman was pals with Myer Baum, called "Bummer Dan" because he was famous for bumming drinks, smokes, chews, and meals from all and sundry. On a late-August night, Sam Young was on duty behind the bar at the No. 10. Hartman gave his own coat to Bummer Dan to wear; opinion is divided whether this was a prank or a ploy. Bummer Dan walked into the No. 10, heading to the bar. Sam Young shot and killed him.

Young, a largely law-abiding sort, was horrified at his mistake and immediately turned himself in to the sheriff. He said it was self-defense; he had fired when he recognized that coat coming toward him.

He was tried for murder, and the jury acquitted him after a few hours' deliberation. Since Jack McCall had just gotten off for Hickok's killing, some citizens were cynical about what a Deadwood newspaper called "the usual verdict."

When October rolled around, and preparations for McCall's second arrest were afoot, Young apparently decided it was time for him to move on before he received the same treatment. To get to the railroad at Cheyenne, he hired on as one of ten guards escorting a wagon filled with a ton of gold dust. He headed to Nevada and then California, eventually settling for life in Portland, Oregon.

Young said that it was dime novels that had inspired him to run away from his New York home when he was fourteen in 1863:

> *I had read everything obtainable in the line of dime novels, and my head was so filled with "hair-raising" stories of Indians, hunters, trappers, and other denizens of the Wild West, that I had my mind made up that it was my duty to go forth and encroach upon the domains of those nomads and assist in the extermination of the Noble Red Man.*

He trapped with an old hand for a while, worked on railroad construction crews, and found other types of laboring jobs as he continued moving westward. Young was in his late teens when he landed in Hays City, Kansas, and "formed a boyish fancy" for one of the dance hall girls. He danced with her all of one night, spending almost all the $40 he'd started the evening with.

Young was waiting outside the dance hall for her to get off work in the morning when a man approached him—Wild Bill Hickok, Young claimed in his book. Hickok struck the youth as kindly and concerned as he revealed that he'd been watching his free spending through the night. "He gave me some very wholesome advice regarding spending my money so foolishly…" (Young wrote that this was in 1868, but Hickok's presence would mean it was 1869.)

When Young said he was looking for work in Hays, Hickok asked whether he could drive a team of mules. After Young answered in the negative, Hickok taught him how to harness a six-mule team in the style government contractors used, then got him a job. Young stayed in Hays for six months, often visiting with his benefactor.

Driving a team for the Jenney expedition of 1875 first brought Sam Young into the Black Hills and also acquainted him with Calamity Jane. Disguised in a cavalry uniform, Jane traveled with a sergeant in the military escort—which lasted only until her presence was discovered and his commander, Colonel Richard Dodge, evicted her from camp and told her to return to Fort Laramie.

It was a trip she didn't want to make alone because of the Sioux war parties that were trying to drive whites out of the Hills, so she asked the teamsters if she could travel with them. She would serve as their cook in return. Young claims that he talked the wagonmaster into accepting, and she often rode on Young's wagon during the rest of the expedition.

When Young once accidentally turned that wagon over and dumped the woman into Spring Creek, he committed one of the most embarrassing mistakes a teamster could make. Calamity Jane increased the insult by assuming he'd done it on purpose and royally cursed him out. Whenever she saw him in the future, she brought up the "time he tried to drown her."

After the Jenney expedition, Young followed the rush to Custer City, where he and a friend established a saloon, "the best equipped one…that was ever conducted" there. After Young turned down appointment as town marshal, he did allow the mayor to name him as deputy. Thus he dealt with Tom Milligan's shooting of his own partner.

Young arrived in Deadwood in 1876, not too long before Hickok, and was already working at the No. 10 Saloon when the two had their reunion. Hickok complimented Carl Mann for hiring Young, saying he was an honest worker. Fewer than three weeks later, Young was tending bar when Hickok was killed there.

RICHARD "BANJO DICK" BROWN
Self-Defense from the Stage
Dick Brown sang the sentimental and humorous ballads of the day, accompanying himself on that low-class instrument deemed suitable only for variety theaters and saloons: the banjo.

In Cheyenne he had met Fannie Garrettson, another musical

performer, and the two fell for each other. The only hindrance to their new bond was that she was living with Ed Shaughnessy, who did not take the news kindly. So Brown and Garrettson headed for Deadwood in 1876—not eloping, just escaping together.

Historian Watson Parker tells that Brown was on stage, late that autumn, at one of Deadwood's variety theaters; accounts disagree about whether it was the Gem, the Bella Union, or the Melodeon. Ed Shaughnessy showed up and, instead of applauding Brown's singing and picking, threw an ax at him. Or perhaps, as some say, it was only a packet of Garrettson's love letters that caught the lights' reflection and looked like a flying ax head.

Brown, of course, was "heeled," or armed—even on stage—and at once emptied his six-shooter into Shaughnessy, killing him. He was also, of course, acquitted of murder because he had many witnesses eager to claim it was self-defense.

Fannie Garrettson defended her reputation, such as it was, by writing to the local papers to explain that she'd never been married to Shaughnessy, so leaving him wasn't a crime.

Some sources say that Brown and Garrettson promptly proceeded to tie the knot, then performed together on a circuit of all of Deadwood's variety theaters.

BOONE MAY
Scourge of the Road Agents

Daniel Boone May, who went by his middle name, was one scary man, possibly the fastest gun in the Black Hills and along the Deadwood-Cheyenne stage road. Rolf Johnson, who met him in the late 1870s, wrote that "he was a man I would instinctively fear without knowing who he was." May's eyes were an unusual "hue between yellow, green, and gray, and had a curious restless look about them."

Luckily for the stage line, Boone May was on their side. He was one of their best shotgun messengers on the Monitor treasure coach, and he also managed Robbers Roost Stage Station at the Cheyenne River. His brother Jim managed the next station to the south, May's Ranch. Born in Missouri (Boone in 1852), the boys had been raised on a Kansas farm.

When Boone May was photographed in his prime, even the black-and-white image revealed his odd—some said scary—eye coloration, which was described as "a hue between yellow, green, and gray." WYOMING STATE ARCHIVES, DEPARTMENT OF STATE PARKS AND CULTURAL RESOURCES, #2461.

Brother Bill, also in the area, sometimes rode with Boone and Jim in outlaw-hunting posses. They began working for the Cheyenne and Black Hills Stage Company in 1877 when it opened a new section of its road to Deadwood.

Before leaving the stage line's employ in 1880, Boone May was recorded as responsible for the deaths of robbers Frank K. Towle, Joe Manuse (shot by May and Billy Sample), William "Curly" Grimes, and at least one unnamed robber, and for the arrests of robbers Prescott Webb, C. P. Wisdom, G. W. Connor, Tom Price, Archie McLaughlin, and William "Billy" Mansfield.

In addition to Boone May's service as shotgun messenger, he was appointed a deputy U.S. marshal in 1878, by special agent John B. Furay of the U.S. Post Office. May also worked part-time as a shotgun messenger for the Black Hills Placer Mining Company during the summer of 1880. He was hired by the firm's general manager, author Ambrose Bierce, who would start publishing his cynically humorous *Devil's Dictionary* as a newspaper series the following year.

Curly Grimes's death in February 1880 led to a charge of murder for May and U.S. Department of Justice special agent W. H. Llewellyn when the bandit's pals claimed the killing was in cold blood. At their August trial, the shooters were acquitted by a jury that didn't even have to leave the jury box to reach their decision.

May was under indictment when Bierce hired him, and the New York capitalists who owned Black Hills Placer Mining objected to the situation. The intransigent Bierce simply amended the payroll, changing May's occupation from "shotgun messenger" to "murderer," and kept him on.

In his article "A Sole Survivor," Bierce gives a glimpse of Boone May in action. One dark and rainy night, the two of them were driving a wagon with $30,000 in Black Hills Placer Mining gold from Deadwood to Rockerville. May had his rifle in a leather scabbard on his lap when the unwanted command came:

> *"Throw up your hands!"*
> *With an involuntary jerk at the reins I brought my team to its haunches and reached for my revolver. Quite*

needless: with the quickest movement that I had ever seen in anything but a cat—almost before the words were out of the horseman's mouth—May had thrown himself backward across the back of the seat, face upward, and the muzzle of his rifle was within a yard of the fellow's breast! What further occurred among the three of us there in the gloom of the forest has, I fancy, never been accurately related. Boone May is long dead of yellow fever in Brazil, and I am the Sole Survivor.

Before and after the trial, Grimes's friends were making plenty of noise about their plans for revenge. When stopping stagecoaches, they inquired if May was aboard, but they never stopped the right one. At one point, May was riding the Deadwood-bound stage from Sidney, Nebraska. When his coach met the southbound stage, its driver told May about being stopped some miles back by bad boys looking for him. May boarded the southbound stage and went right on back to Sidney.

By the time May and Llewellyn's trial was over, the gold rush was fading and Boone May apparently decided he no longer needed the aggravation of looking over his shoulder for Grimes's pals. He left the Hills and apparently moved on to Chile three years later. In 1891, he and an army officer had eyes for the same señorita, and the officer ended up dead. May fled to the gold fields of Brazil, where he died from an illness, not a gunshot, in the early 1900s.

TWO MURDER/SUICIDES
In the Name of Love

Charley Wilson & Kitty Clide

Estelline Bennett, in *Old Deadwood Days*, tells the story of a murder that incensed her parents. Judge Granville Bennett knew and respected the killer's father as a solid, hardworking man and was extremely dismayed at what the son had come to.

Charley Wilson and his father arrived in the Black Hills in 1876, and by 1880 Charley was playing in the Gem Theater's orchestra. He fell in love with one of the waiter girls, whose name Ms. Bennett gives as Kitty Clide The lovers were alone together in a Gem Theater upstairs room in the wee hours one summer night when Charley shot and killed Kitty, then shot himself.

Historian Jerry Bryant, who has extensively researched the story, notes that Kitty and Charley had known each other in Chicago, where Al Swearingen recruited her for the Gem. Charley followed her west, thinking they were a permanent pair. But that evening, after painting the new schoolhouse all day, Charley turned up at the Gem and found Kitty with another man. He went to his room, retrieved his gun, and returned to end his and Kitty's lives.

When others ran into the room, they found Charley still alive, and he explained that he'd shot Kitty because he loved her so much. His own wound was diagnosed as non-fatal, and his father took him home to recover. The heartbroken young man lingered for two weeks before succumbing to his own bullet, and he never stopped explaining that he'd done it all for love.

As Bennett puts it, not even the low-down denizens of the badlands entertainment district "sympathized with his manner of expressing affection."

Sam Curley & Kitty Leroy

It was a case of blaming the victim, according to Estelline Bennett, when Sam Curley killed his wife, Kitty Leroy, and then himself.

Bennett's informant was making the point that gamblers like Curley never committed suicide when their luck turned sour. That they took as just the cost of doing business. Honest gamblers always paid their debts, and so their credit was good to keep playing until their luck turned again. Only love could cause a gambler's suicide, Bennett's friend claimed.

Sam Curley was a faro dealer who had left his wife, Kitty, in Deadwood while he hit the road. She worked as a "jig dancer" in one of the variety theaters. Whether they considered the marriage over, no one knows.

But Curley came back to Deadwood unexpectedly on December 6, 1877. Kitty was staying in a rented room upstairs from the Lone Star Saloon. Even though his surprise arrival found her alone in her digs, he accused her of unfaithfulness by way of a greeting, then killed her and himself.

WILLIAM (BILL) GAY
Generous Frontiersman Gone Bad

William (Bill) Gay did pretty well for himself in the Black Hills, where he married a Sioux woman named Owns The Mule and lived with Spotted Tail's band. He sold illegal whiskey to his Indian friends and family and served some jail time for it. When he left Deadwood after helping found it in 1876 at the age of thirty-two, he'd made a fortune of $100,000.

Gay dressed like a successful businessman rather than in frontier buckskins or miners' denims. He wore fresh white shirts, and his vest sported a watch chain that was two feet long, made of gold nuggets as big as hickory nuts, with a couple of even larger ones dangling from it.

He was said to be generous to both friends and strangers who were down on their luck, and he claimed, "I have risked my life a hundred times or more to save people from harm, people I never saw before, or since, but that don't count for anything among the race today."

Not far from Deadwood, Bill and his brother Al had founded the town of Gayville shortly before Deadwood came to be. The first saloon and dance hall combination was theirs, because they had figured out how to make money more easily than in the backbreaking line of gold mining.

Mrs. Gay and their daughter, Maud, also were Gayville residents. Therein lay Bill's first problem, when a miner named Lloyd Forbes became a little too admiring of Mrs. Gay in 1877. Bill responded by shooting and killing Forbes, then claimed it was a mere accident. The jury agreed—somewhat. After being convicted of second-degree manslaughter, Gay was sent off to Detroit to serve his time (both Dakota and Wyoming territories contracted with other jurisdictions to house prisoners when their territorial prisons were overfilled), and Dakota's territorial supreme court refused to hear his appeal.

Historian Jerry Bryant says that Gay's wife "haunted the territorial governor" until she got her husband released. His fortune gone for legal fees, he then filed on a Spearfish-area homestead in 1882.

The family moved to Castle, Montana, in 1889, where Bill got sideways of the local newspaper. He built his home on land the newspaper's publisher claimed; when the paper's building burned down, some Castle residents suspected Gay. A message threatening vigilante action was

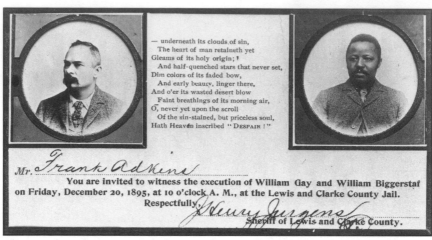

This rare formal invitation to a hanging shows William Gay on the left. By this appointed date, Gay had what proved a temporary stay of execution, and murderer William Biggerstaf, whose crime was unrelated, was hanged alone.
MONTANA HISTORICAL SOCIETY.

tacked to the door of the Gays' home, and the family moved away.

In 1893, they were living on the Musselshell River in central Montana when lawmen came to serve a warrant on Bill and his brother-in-law, Harry Gross. The pair were accused of thefts in Wyoming. Answering the process servers with gunfire, they escaped arrest, but the posse returned to try again. This time lawmen shot Gay in the leg, and when Deputy Bill Rader moved toward him, Gross shot and killed the deputy. Gay and Gross both escaped again.

The third time was almost a charm for arresting Bill Gay, but this time another deputy, James Macke, was fatally wounded. During the two days he lingered, Macke repeatedly said it was Gay, not Gross, who shot him. Again both gunmen escaped—Gross for good. But someone recognized Bill Gay in California two years later. He was arrested, returned to Montana, and tried in the capital city of Helena on the theory that its jury pool would be untainted with opinions about the killings far away on the Musselshell River.

Even though Gay claimed he was innocent of Macke's killing—practically to the moment of his death—he was hanged in Helena's county jail on June 9, 1896.

CHAPTER FOUR

ROBBERS, RUSTLERS & PLAIN OLD THIEVES

TRIPLE ROBBERIES & SOME MURDERS

The Gang of Five Plus Their Pals

On the nights of June 25, 26, and 27, 1877, a gang robbed stagecoaches near the Black Hills Trail's Cheyenne River crossing. None of the vehicles was a treasure coach, so the gang netted only about $1,700 in cash and jewelry. On the second night, the road agents pulled out the treasure box on the southbound coach and blew it open, but it proved to be empty. They also shot the driver, luckily for him only grazing his side. The next night they took an unrecorded amount of money from the treasure box. They told the driver to demand that the company place loose treasure boxes in the coaches, instead of bolting them down, to save time for robbers like themselves. And, furthermore, if some treasure from Custer City didn't start showing up, they'd go burn down that town!

According to Robert "Little Reddy" McKimie, the five masked men were: Clark Pelton (aka "Billy Webster"), Dunc Blackburn, James Wall, Bill Bevans, and McKimie himself. An unnamed woman also was traveling with the group.

Robert "Little Reddy" McKimie

Robert McKimie's red hair and impudent, impulsive attitude earned him the nickname Little Reddy, as in always ready for anything. His lifelong pattern seemed to be working in a respectable job for a while, then returning to the bad boy business. Before he arrived in the Black Hills he'd served time in the Utah territorial prison for stage robbery. In 1875, he was a popular handyman at the grand Inter Ocean Hotel in Cheyenne—until the manager fired him for mouthing off one too many times.

Reddy McKimie moved on to the Black Hills, first attracting Sheriff Seth Bullock's attention by trying to sell a stolen horse at too good a bargain price. Bullock jailed him, the owner got his horse back, and McKimie was released because the ad hoc government didn't want to waste the money on trial expenses. McKimie continued with his life of crime, joining the Collins-Bass gang early in 1877.

Joel Collins, Sam Bass, Frank Towle, McKimie, and another man struck the Deadwood-bound stagecoach on March 25, 1877. Up on the boot that night was twenty-six-year-old John H. "Johnny" Slaughter, the Cheyenne and Black Hills Stage Company's best driver. Slaughter was a popular fellow, with large circles of friends in both Deadwood and Cheyenne. He was the son of Cheyenne's city marshal, John N. Slaughter (not related to "Texas" John Slaughter, a lawman in the Southwest). Walter Iler, a traveling salesman for an Omaha distillery, was riding beside Johnny Slaughter on the boot.

Slaughter was driving hard to make up lost time after some delays at Hill City. When the road agents brought the stage to a halt in Whitewood Canyon, McKimie was standing near the lead horses, the first of three pairs pulling the coach. The overheated animals were nervous and started moving about, so McKimie fired his shotgun, putting a circle of buckshot around Slaughter's heart, a few pieces of shot into Iler's arm, and another through the coat sleeve of a second passenger.

Canadian-born Seth Bullock had been a Montana territorial senator, sheriff, and merchant before he and partner Sol Star moved their hardware store to Deadwood. He later was a Rough Rider officer under Teddy Roosevelt. ADAMS MUSEUM AND HOUSE, INC., DEADWOOD, SOUTH DAKOTA.

The horses bolted at the sound, and Slaughter fell off the boot either dead or dying. Iler managed to get control of the coach and guide it into Deadwood around midnight. An irate posse immediately set out and brought in Johnny Slaughter's body.

(Just to confuse matters, Calamity Jane later inserted herself into the action in her false autobiography, claiming that Indians attacked and that she was the one who calmed the horses and drove the coach into Deadwood—with the body of Johnny Slaughter aboard.)

After the easy placer gold was gone, miners tunneled underground, as shown here at the Deadwood Gulch discovery site, which is located in Deadwood's business district.
COURTESY NATIONAL ARCHIVES, NWDNS-165-2F-10.

Deadwood residents held a funeral service for Slaughter, and his body was taken home to Cheyenne. For the funeral there, the city's largest to date, stage line manager Luke Voorhees supplied six matched white horses to pull the hearse. Johnny Slaughter was buried on April 4, 1877, with his mother—a woman in her mid-fifties—following him in death just over three weeks later.

Now the Collins-Bass gang members had $500 prices on their heads, and they were furious with McKimie. When they learned that one of the passengers had been carrying $15,000, which they would have found if he hadn't fired his shotgun, they seriously discussed killing Little Reddy. Somehow, they decided instead to kick him out of the gang. They told him to leave the Black Hills as well, but that was advice he didn't take.

Instead, he connected with Blackburn, Pelton, Wall, and Bevans. Three months later, that gang pulled off their triple robberies on the three June nights.

After the robberies, the group soon proved that there is no honor among thieves. McKimie and Pelton traveled to South Pass, in Wyoming Territory, to stock up on supplies. While they were gone, the woman heard the others planning to kill them when they returned and warned McKimie when he got back.

Together with Bevans, McKimie and Pelton got the plotters drunk, then stole $8,000 worth of gold and nearly all the folding money. McKimie and the woman rode south to the Union Pacific rail line and caught a train for St. Louis. After McKimie gave her $1,000 for saving his life, he went east, selling his ill-gotten gold to the Philadelphia mint and then going home to Hillsboro, Ohio. There he married his sweetheart and told people he'd gotten rich as a cattleman out west.

He first bought a farm, then exchanged it for a store. Amazingly, word of where Reddy McKimie was got back to Deadwood. The next January, Sheriff Bullock took the train east and made his way to Hillsboro. As soon as he arrested McKimie, the robber drew on his ill-gotten fortune to hire good lawyers and fight extradition, so Bullock telegraphed Luke Voorhees to come help him. As Voorhees headed east, McKimie confessed and named his cohorts.

Even with this confession, Hillsboro law officers apparently didn't take the western officers' claims too seriously. They had been taken in by McKimie's "solid citizen" act. While McKimie stayed in jail and his lawyers filed papers, his wife and friends were free to come and go from the jail as they pleased, never being searched. In mid-February, McKimie escaped—had someone smuggled in a gun for him? For a year he committed robberies in Ohio and Kentucky before being arrested and jailed. He apparently never returned to the Black Hills.

Bill Bevans

Bill Bevans had been a Montana rancher, but he lost everything through gambling. After stealing a horse from a Wyoming rancher, he had been arrested the year before the triple robberies and jailed in Laramie. Facing a ten-year jail sentence, he appealed—then escaped with Dunc Blackburn and Clark Pelton and joined their gang.

He was the first of the gang of five to be arrested, at Lander, Wyoming Territory, not long after the three June 1877 robberies. Bevans was found carrying a gold watch taken from a passenger during one of them. Even though he tried to break out of the Cheyenne jail that July, he went to trial and on to the penitentiary, where he stayed until 1886. He died soon after he was released.

Clark Pelton

Early in July 1877, just days after the three night robberies, Deputy Sheriff Charles Hays of Fort Laramie heard that Clark Pelton and Dunc Blackburn were at the Six Mile Stage Station, not far away. He stopped at the Three Mile station and deputized co-owner Adolph Cuny and a man named Sprague to help him with an arrest. Arriving at Six Mile, the group captured Pelton and Blackburn, then left Cuny to guard them while searching the station for the other robbers. Pelton shot and killed Cuny. He and Blackburn eventually escaped to Fort Pierre, where they split up.

Pelton soon had a new partner in crime: Laughing Sam Hartman. They pulled a few jobs along the Deadwood stagecoach road, hitting freight wagons and stagecoaches and also stealing horses from stage stations and ranches. After they'd put together more than $4,000, they decided to hide out for a while.

The pair went to Iowa and hired on with a farmer for laborers' wages, and they buried their money on his land. After things quieted down, they planned to return to the lucrative stage road. But the world was smaller than they thought, as we see in Laughing Sam's story, below.

After the pair were arrested and tried, Pelton ended up serving one year in the Minnesota penitentiary for robbery, but when he walked out a free man in 1879, Laramie County (Wyoming) sheriff George W. Draper was waiting to arrest him for killing Cuny. Pelton was then convicted of manslaughter, sentenced to one to four years, and taken right back to the penitentiary.

Samuel S. "Laughing Sam" Hartman

When Laughing Sam Hartman teamed up with Clark Pelton for some stage robberies, it may have been a career change for the sometime faro dealer. After the pair's success in late 1877, they traveled to Iowa together, where they buried the loot. However lucky Hartman may have been up until then, as a robber and gambler, his luck now deserted him.

One day a neighboring farmer came along the road and saw the two fellows working away. This neighbor had recently been to the Black Hills, where he'd been robbed while riding a stagecoach. Oh, yes—and he recognized Hartman. Even though it was a nighttime robbery, this man had held a gun to the neighbor's head while taking his money and jewelry.

In that friendly Iowa way, the neighbor stopped and chatted with the workers for a while, then went straight to local lawmen and told them to watch Hartman and make sure he didn't leave the area. After that, the neighbor went to Omaha to inform federal authorities, who promptly arrested both Hartman and Pelton and transported them to Rapid City for trial. Pelton received only a one-year sentence for the robberies, but Hartman—with testimony about the gun to the head—was sentenced to eight years for highway robbery.

As a gambler before he turned robber, Hartman had already been a shady character when he ran a faro bank in Deadwood. A prostitute with the professional name of Tid Bit played at his bank one time, receiving her winnings in gold dust. When the dust turned out to be brass filings mixed with black sand, she complained to her friends.

Now, Tid Bit had had the good luck to travel to Deadwood in the Hickok-Utter train, so Calamity Jane was one of the people who heard how Hartman had cheated her friend. She borrowed two pistols from Charlie Utter and faced down the gambler, cursing him out as colorfully as she could—which, witnesses always reported, was pretty colorfully.

Hartman promptly set things right by giving Tid Bit two $20 gold pieces, the real thing from Uncle Sam.

Dunc Blackburn & James Wall

After Reddy McKimie and the unnamed woman ran off in 1877—but before Clark Pelton killed Adolph Cuny—Dunc Blackburn, James

Wall, and Pelton continued robbing coaches in the Cheyenne River crossing area.

They had plenty of competition. That summer of 1877 was the height of the Black Hills gold rush, and plenty of robbers were stopping stagecoaches, day after day, on the Black Hills Trail's northern portion. On the night of July 17, the southbound coach had to halt twice—meeting two different gangs only twelve miles apart. The first set of bad boys got the gold and jewelry, so the second group took blankets and guns. The northbound coach also was robbed on the same night, but people heading *to* the Hills tended not to have as much to offer, and those robbers grabbed only $13.

After Cuny's murder, the gang moved south toward Laramie. A posse searching for Blackburn and Pelton, which included Cheyenne sheriff T. Jeff Carr and five soldiers from Fort D. A. Russell, received reports of sightings as they rode. The newspapers covered their manhunt, so when Blackburn went into Laramie for supplies, he read about the posse on his own trail.

The three robbers got away to Fort Pierre, and Pelton moved on from there (soon to be arrested). Now Dunc Blackburn partnered with James Wall, and they returned to the Deadwood-Cheyenne stage road.

On September 26, Scott "Quick Shot" Davis and John Denny were shotgun messengers on the treasure coach that left Deadwood. Alex Benham, a stage line division manager who had just been transferred to Deadwood, was aboard, along with a company stock tender. The coach stopped at Jenney Stockade to pick up some soldiers, who rode inside.

When the coach reached the deep grass of the Cheyenne River bottom, the men heard the order to halt. Davis and Denny jumped down, their guns cocked. They were pretty much on their own. The soldiers and stock tender fled, leaving their guns inside at the robbers' demand. One of the soldiers knocked Davis's rifle from his hands, and while he grabbed for it Denny began firing.

Quickly rearmed, Davis spied one robber lying in the grass and shot him, receiving a wound to his right thigh in return. Manager Benham and the driver held onto the horses' harness to keep them from running off during the gunfire.

Despite his wound, Davis realized that the two black-masked robbers had been calling him by name, which meant that they must be known in Deadwood. They took Denny's pocket watch and a small revolver Benham had in one pocket. Davis talked them into giving back the watch, since Denny was just an employee doing his job.

By then, the soldiers and stock tender had returned, hands in the air, shouting their surrender. Now that the robbers were in control, they admitted they thought they'd been robbing a regular coach, not the treasure run, and had hoped for money and jewelry from passengers. As long as the coach is stopped, they asked, how about letting us have a look at that fancy safe you're carrying? After inspecting it, they took off.

The robbers were Blackburn and Wall, who soon were bragging about the event.

The Cheyenne and Black Hills Stage Company immediately put out a reward for both men: $1,000 for their arrest and conviction, or $200 apiece if they were dead. Laramie County offered $200 each, dead or alive, for any man who had robbed a coach in July or August of 1877. This was in addition to the standing offer of $200 for any road agent, dead or alive, put up by the Lawrence County commissioners in Deadwood.

The stage company also put in its order for a customized treasure coach, the Monitor, which went into service the following year.

Still, Blackburn and Wall kept meeting success in the autumn of 1877, hitting coaches as miners left the Hills before winter. In early October, they probably robbed a coach only twelve miles from the "protection" of Fort Laramie. Besides what they took from passengers, they broke open the treasure box, but it contained only documents, which they left behind.

On October 9, Blackburn and Wall robbed both the southbound and northbound coaches, taking blankets and even underwear in addition to cash and valuables. They even made the sole woman take down her hair, having gotten wise to this trick of female stage passengers. Sure enough, Mrs. Ella King had stashed some money in her upswept hairdo.

Stage passenger John H. "Jack" Bowman, who ran the Hat Creek Stage Station, immediately recognized the voice of Blackburn, a former employee of his. Both robbers unmasked, refused to take his money, and offered Bowman a drink of whiskey.

Then the bad boys wanted to know what was being said about the frequent robberies, and who was thought to be doing them. Bowman told them that they were, and further that a company of soldiers was looking for them. Wall exhibited his cockiness by replying, as Bowman recalled, "Wish they would put a company of cavalry on our trail—we could make some money out of their horses."

Soon a rancher told Crook City officers that he'd seen Wall in that vicinity, so a posse headed out on the road toward Crook City and Bismarck. When the posse spotted a stagecoach robbery in progress, the bad boys fled.

Deadwood's sheriff, Seth Bullock, was getting frustrated over the elusive Blackburn and Wall, so he and some of his men hid out near Crook City that night. When two men on horseback started into town around midnight, Bullock demanded they stop. One of his deputies' guns went off accidentally, and in the confusion the pair got away, high-tailing it south to the Cheyenne River. It turned out that the two were indeed the robbers, and Blackburn had received two gunshot wounds in his arm.

Bullock was up for reelection as sheriff, and his inability to nab Blackburn and Wall became quite a campaign issue. Though he would go on to a long career as a U.S. marshal, Bullock was defeated at the polls that November, after only one term as sheriff. John Manning became Deadwood's new sheriff.

The reason Bullock failed to capture Blackburn and Wall was that they had run west across Wyoming, herding eight horses stolen from the stagecoach company along the Oregon Trail and crossing the Rocky Mountains at South Pass. From there, they headed toward Green River in southwestern Wyoming, eventually stopping to rest at Alkali Stage Station. Surely, they thought, distance and winter weather had prevented lawmen from following.

However, as historian Agnes Wright Spring recounts, they did not count on the tenacity of Scott "Quick Shot" Davis, the shotgun messenger captain wounded in September, who was back on the job in November. With soldiers from Fort Laramie, he tracked the horse herd across Wyoming while the snows fell. Near South Pass City, the soldiers claimed their horses were worn out and refused to continue. Davis proceeded alone, eventually having to leave his horse, carry his saddle, and take a stagecoach toward Green River.

When Davis's coach pulled into the Alkali station, he described the fugitives to the manager, who claimed he hadn't seen them. But a woman employee promptly said two men fitting that description were currently sleeping in the haystack.

Davis sprang outside and spotted Blackburn and Wall's bedrolls in the moonlight. As soon as he shouted that they were under arrest, both outlaws began shooting and fleeing. Davis returned fire, hitting Wall in both legs. Blackburn, bootless and coatless, escaped.

Quick Shot Davis collected the stolen horses and found one of his own guns—stolen during a robbery—in the haystack.

Sending Wall in the custody of a local deputy to Green River, Davis drove the horses into town. At once, he passed around Blackburn's description to lawmen and the public. That night a shivering man walked into a store—with no hat or coat, his feet wrapped in underwear. Another customer notified Davis and the local police.

Soon Blackburn came out of the store dressed more suitably for winter weather and went on to a restaurant. A deputy arrested him, politely waiting until he finished dinner. Blackburn did not put up a fight, having hidden his gun outside town.

Davis and the two bad boys rode the Union Pacific trail to Cheyenne, with the horses aboard in a boxcar, arriving on November 23.

In Cheyenne, both men were convicted of highway robbery, assault with intent to murder, grand larceny, and obstructing the mail. Each was sentenced to a total of eight years in the Wyoming territorial prison and assessed a fine of $99.

James Wall Spares an Old Friend

Before he arrived in Custer City and Deadwood, bartender Sam Young had been a teamster. Before James Wall turned to robbing stages, he also drove teams—and at one time the pair worked for the same company for two years.

Late in the spring of 1876, Young had to travel from Deadwood south to

Custer City, carrying $500 in paper currency—"greenbacks." When the stage left that night, Young found his fellow passengers to be a dance hall girl, a heavy-drinking man who'd installed Deadwood's telegraph line and earned the sobriquet "Telegraphy," and four other men. At midnight, all were napping when the coach stopped at the feared road agent greeting, "Hands up."

One robber with a shotgun and another holding two revolvers had the passengers step down. They wore no masks, and Young was surprised to recognize his one-time co-worker, James Wall. Wall went through the men's pockets, ignoring the woman, and when he reached Telegraphy announced that he knew the man wasn't making a trip without a bottle of whiskey. Telegraphy said it was under the seat cushion, and Wall grabbed it out of the coach. Then Wall, fearing a trick, told Telegraphy to take a drink to prove the bottle wasn't "doped" with chloral hydrate. Telegraphy was only too glad to oblige and took a good, long pull before Wall snatched the bottle away.

Reaching Sam Young, Wall recognized his former friend. Young later wrote, "Wall looked at me for a moment and playfully tapping me under the chin with his six-shooter, remarked in a low tone, 'I see, old pal, you are also caught in the net!' But he did not molest me."

The road agents released the coach, telling the driver to go on without looking back. Seated inside again, Young found that the rest of the passengers now assumed he was somehow a confederate of the robbers. When he explained himself, Telegraphy believed him and managed to convince the others.

SAM BASS & JOEL COLLINS
Texas Robbers Take On the Black Hills Stage

Sam Bass, from Indiana, was orphaned in 1864, when he was thirteen years old, and lived among relatives for the next five years before heading off to Texas. For a couple of years he made money by owning an excellent racehorse, and then he turned to cowboying. Bass and a fellow named Joel Collins put together a cattle drive with stock from several owners and headed north to the Kansas markets. When the cattle were sold and the cowboys paid, Bass and Collins held $8,000 in proceeds.

Unfortunately, they forgot about paying the owners—and went on a fine gambling spree until the money ran out. So in 1876, they headed to the Black Hills.

At first Bass and Collins tried honest work, prospecting in the Deadwood area and then organizing a small freighting company. But the contents of stagecoaches—and their passengers' pockets—soon proved more attractive. The Collins-Bass gang was credited with seven coach robberies in 1877, but they never made a big score.

Robbing railroad trains, which carried mail and payroll cash as well as more passengers with pockets and handbags to clean out, had been "invented" in 1867 by some other Indiana bad boys and perfected by the James gang beginning in 1872. Collins and Bass left the Black Hills and turned their eyes to the regional railway goliath, the Union Pacific.

On September 18, 1877, they stopped the Union Pacific train at Big Springs, Nebraska, ten miles east of the Colorado border. Heading east, the train had a cargo of brand-new $20 gold pieces from the San Francisco mint, $60,000 worth of them. When the Collins-Bass gang claimed the gold, it was their personal biggest haul ever, and this robbery would hold the record as the Union Pacific's greatest such loss. As a bonus, the gang took $1,300 and gold jewelry from the passengers. Then they temporarily split up to hide.

Within a couple of weeks, Joel Collins was killed by lawmen trying to arrest him. Bass escaped, went to Texas, and created a new gang. Because this Sam Bass gang became famous for robbing banks, stagecoaches, and trains in Texas, his earlier Black Hills gang is always referred to as the Collins-Bass gang. After returning to Texas, though, Bass never took his new gang north to the Hills.

Although the Sam Bass gang was active in Texas, these bad boys never collected much money, and they lasted only until the following summer. The Texas Rangers pinned them down in a July 19, 1878, shootout after the gang robbed the Round Rock bank. Bass was wounded and died two days later, on his twenty-seventh birthday.

JACK BOWMAN & JACK BOWMAN
Bad Boy at Six Mile, Good One at Hat Creek
The summer of 1877, there were two Jack Bowmans: the bad Jack and

the good Jack. Jack Bowman tended the Six Mile Stage Station. Word went around that he aided and abetted robbers who stopped by his place, and the Cheyenne and Black Hills Stage Company replaced him with Curly Coleman.

Just to complicate matters, the tender at the Hat Creek Stage Station at this time was John H. Bowman, who also went by the nickname Jack. But he was a good stage line employee and was often deputized to join posses hunting bad boys.

The good Jack Bowman had quite a spread: 200 acres with a primitive hotel; post and telegraph offices; brewery, bakery, and butcher shop; blacksmith to fix wagons and coaches; and grain, hay, and stables for the horses. His wife, Sallie, helped run the hotel and fed those who stopped for meals. They sold the Hat Creek station for a considerable price to freighter Charles Hecht in 1879 and moved away.

PRESCOTT WEBB
Shooting It Out in the Street
Three men who had arrived in Deadwood after driving cattle north from Texas started their lives in the Black Hills with hard, honest work. Prescott Webb, G. W. Connor, and C. P. Wisdom worked as bullwhackers and then as wild-game hunters, camping out as they followed the game, then selling the meat in Deadwood. But then they turned to stagecoach robbery.

When the trio stopped the Cheyenne-bound stagecoach one August night in 1877, they found a woman and her child, two gamblers, and shotgun messenger Boone May. The last was ready to fight, but the woman put up such a protest that May became angry, threw his fine rifle out the window, and told the robbers to take what they wanted. Prescott Webb claimed the rifle.

Webb, Wisdom, and Connor discussed shooting May on the spot and getting rid of one of the road agents' worst enemies. However, they decided against murder.

May was so frustrated because he and the gamblers, Mike Goldman and Jim Lebby, were riding together on purpose, hoping to catch road agents that night. When the woman and child started to board the coach in Deadwood, May demanded that the driver make her take the coach another day, but he lost the argument.

A couple of weeks later, Boone May was walking down the street in Deadwood when he spied Prescott Webb. As soon as the robber saw him, he started firing his two revolvers. Even though he hit May in the left wrist before grabbing someone's horse for a getaway, May shot both the horse and Webb, the latter under the shoulder blade. Webb continued down the street a short distance before he was surrounded by Sheriff Seth Bullock, Deputy John Cochrane, and A. M. Willard, who arrested him.

Webb apparently gave up his two partners, because they joined him in jail later the same day. C. P. Wisdom kept insisting they'd come into Deadwood only to sell their last wild meat before leaving the Hills, but his promise to go away did no good.

Now it was their turn for a stagecoach ride—a one-way ticket to Cheyenne under the care of Deputy J. W. Murray. They even had an escort of soldiers for the Cheyenne River crossing portion of the road. After they were arraigned, the three novice road agents sat in jail because they had no money to pay their own bail.

CORNELIUS "LAME JOHNNY" DONAHUE
A Fresh Start Goes Sour
Soft-spoken, educated, and well dressed, John A. Hurley made a good impression on Cheyenne freighter John Francis Murphy in 1876. Hurley, in his early twenties, said he'd come from Philadelphia and wanted to work his way to the Black Hills. He walked with a limp and had one boot heel built up to compensate for a shortened leg, but Murphy hired him in a minute.

After earning his passage, Hurley prospected throughout the summer, but as winter loomed he went to work as a bookkeeper at the Homestake Mine in Lead. Life was going along quietly and well until a Texan recognized "Hurley" and told management that he was Lame Johnny Donahue (actually Cornelius Donahue), wanted in Texas for horse theft.

The quiet young man then returned to a life of crime, first stealing horses and later adding stage robbery to his resume.

That life wasn't the one intended for him when he was accepted into Philadelphia's Girard College. Endowed by one of the nation's first private bankers, the "college" was a residential school for poor white boys, giving them a home and a solid education until they reached the age of eighteen—thus Johnny's bookkeeping skills. (Girard College continues today, on its original campus and with the same mission of housing and educating low-income students through grade and high school, but now it is co-ed and racially integrated.)

When Johnny was eighteen and had to leave Girard in 1871, he went to Texas and started cowboying. Horse theft by Indians was an ongoing problem, so part of the cowboys' work was stealing their employers' horses back from the Comanches. Thus, Lame Johnny was trained in the fine art of horse theft in the course of a legitimate job.

His employer assisted the young man in starting up his own herd, letting him earn cattle on shares. After Comanches got the entire herd, Johnny claimed that he spent the rest of his life just trying to get back the stake he once had—but no longer using honest ways.

He also liked the excitement and adventure of lawlessness as he turned full-time to his new life. When either the law or vigilantes started looking for him, Johnny decided to move north, and eventually he found his way to Cheyenne and the Black Hills in 1876.

After he left the Homestake Mine, he went back to horse theft. The government herds on the Sioux reservation were attractive targets, and Johnny and his boys had a mysterious way of taking many head at once, then seeming to disappear.

How he did that wasn't known for more than forty years—and then a homesteading couple who discovered Johnny's secret didn't tell anyone for many more years.

Sometime after these homesteaders settled near Lame Johnny Creek in 1919, one of their few, precious steers wandered off on a snowy day. Following its tracks, the man, Orval Halstead, discovered a hidden entrance to a box canyon. Inside the canyon he found two caves. The larger one obviously had been used as a horse corral for, he estimated, as many as thirty horses. In the smaller one, he found men's clothing, boots, bedding, and a well-used fireplace.

Orval told no one but his wife, and she didn't share the story until the 1960s, adding that they always thought the caves were Lame Johnny's hideout. Today, hikers in Custer State Park can still seek them out.

Once stagecoaches began traveling the Black Hills Trail, Johnny wasn't content with horseflesh alone. He and his boys started robbing passenger coaches while continuing their horse thefts. His gang included Frank Harris, Tom Moore, "Little Brocky" (whose real name is lost), a man named Bradley, and George "Tony Pastor" Howard—an interesting alias, since entrepreneur Tony Pastor was then active in New York City, creating vaudeville and hiring the likes of Lillian Russell and George M. Cohan.

In August 1877, Johnny and the boys held up the stage from Deadwood to Sidney, Nebraska, near Buffalo Gap, at a stream since known as Lame Johnny Creek. Stage line division agent Ed Cooke was aboard, holding a child on his lap, when road agents stopped the coach. After the robbers demanded that the passengers step down, Cooke didn't move fast enough, so a robber fired his gun, zinging Cooke on the ear.

Once outside, Cooke recognized Lame Johnny. Even though he put out the word to the stage line's shotgun messengers, it was two years before the elusive Johnny, along with Frank Harris, was arrested around Fort Robinson, Nebraska. They'd stolen horses from a Custer City–area rancher, and James L. "Whispering" Smith, a Laramie County lawman who sometimes worked as a Union Pacific detective, wired Fort Robinson officials to hold them for him to pick up.

Smith escorted the pair on the northbound Sidney-Deadwood stagecoach until they reached the Red Cloud Agency station. Then shotgun messenger Jesse Brown took over custody of the prisoners, riding inside along with his own wife and two children while Smith sat up on the boot with the driver.

After a few miles, Lame Johnny caught sight of the feared Boone May riding alongside the coach and truly began to worry about his fate. When the coach reached Buffalo Gap, Smith moved back inside and Brown mounted a horse to ride behind. Having left that station behind, the coach was soon stopped by eight masked men.

They demanded custody of Lame Johnny, but Smith jumped out to argue. The vigilantes took his revolvers and threw them into the brush, then grabbed Johnny, demanding that he confess and name the others in his gang.

Johnny fought back, yelling to Smith to lend him a gun to defend himself, but to no avail. He contented himself with refusing to betray his pals and was told he'd be hanged if he didn't. Johnny replied, "Hang and be damned; you can't do it any too soon." The vigilantes obliged, despite the presence of Mrs. Brown and her children, who clung to their father as soon as he and his horse caught up.

Some of the ranchers Lame Johnny had victimized are said to have posted a wooden grave marker, long since gone, which said:

> Pilgrim, Pause. You're standing on
> The moldering clay of "Limping John."
> Tread lightly, stranger, on his sod
> For if he moves, you're robbed by G-d.

FRANK WARREN
A Thieving Host Gets More Than Just Desserts

When a newcomer to the Black Hills arrived in Deadwood late in June 1878, he soon thought he had a new friend in Frank Warren. The pair drank together for two solid days, then the newcomer went to Warren's home. After the newcomer fell asleep, though, the hospitality reversed itself, and Warren "went through his pockets, stealing about $16 in money, all he had," according to the *Black Hills Times*.

> On June 26, the victim woke up to a hangover and empty pockets. He soon tracked down Warren and took his revenge by stabbing the robber in the stomach and pulling the blade up toward Warren's breastbone.

A doctor was able to stitch up Warren's wound. Then Calamity Jane stayed with him until amazingly he recovered—one of many times she nursed the sick or injured. This event caused the *Times* to comment: "There's a lot of humanity in Calamity, and she is deserving of much praise for the part she has taken in the particular case."

WHOOPUP CANYON ROBBERY
Passengers Fight Back

John H. "Johnny" Brown

The passenger stage headed from Deadwood to Cheyenne on the night of July 2, 1878, was driven by John Flaherty. In Whoopup Canyon, west of Hill City and east of today's Newcastle, Wyoming, Flaherty got the order to halt. Two road agents, Johnny Brown and Charles Henry Borris, came into view. A third robber, Charley Ross, hid nearby in the brush.

Flaherty's passengers that night were a woman and five men, one of them—Daniel Finn—a one-time Union Pacific Railroad conductor. They stepped down from the coach and began surrendering their money and jewelry.

Finn wasn't having any of it, though. When Brown approached him, the trainman drew his gun and shot at the bad boy, who flattened himself on the ground. Then, firing upward from his hiding place, Charley Ross gave Finn a painful and disfiguring wound to the mouth and nose. He also shot another man in the leg and a third in the thigh. None of the wounds was fatal.

The robbers, including Brown, got away. Flaherty took his wounded passengers to Hat Creek Stage Station, where they could get help, and drove on to Cheyenne.

Johnny Brown's wound became infected while his companions trundled him to Deadwood, where they then waited more than a week before summoning Lurline Monte Verde to attend to him. She pulled him through.

By the end of September, Brown was working for his former victim—the Cheyenne and Black Hills Stage Company. Suspecting him as a robber, the company was willing to hire him in order to keep track of his comings and goings. Four days after the Canyon Springs robbery of September 26, Brown was arrested and taken to Cheyenne. He confessed to being in on the Whoopup Canyon robbery but claimed he had nothing to do with Canyon Springs—an important distinction, because the latter had included a fatality.

George W. Keating & Orbean Davis

Some of the men who answered the call of the Black Hills gold rush figured on making their fortunes from the miners' needs. Among these were ranchers who established their spreads on excellent rangeland extending out from the Hills.

The Spearfish Valley was one such ranching center, but by the summer of 1878 it was plagued with rustlers. They were happy to attend to the miners' need for beef, but without going through all that messy and constant work. With minimal law enforcement available, the ranchers took matters in their own hands and set up a vigilance committee.

The vigilantes had a few disreputable targets in mind. One was George W. Keating, who ran a butcher shop in Central City. Somehow he kept ending up with stolen cattle—a great way to cut down your costs if you're in the meat-processing business. And when he had a temporary oversupply problem, Keating was happy to sell the extra beeves—at really good prices—to competing butchers.

This is apparently just what he was doing one day when a rancher came in the front door of the butcher shop Keating was visiting, and Keating ran out the back. It seems his surplus beef-on-the-hoof had once belonged to that very rancher.

Another fellow the vigilantes were very interested in was Orbean Davis, whose spread was on Spearfish Mountain, even though he worked at a Gayville corral. The mountain was known to be a meeting and sheltering place for area rustlers, a convenience the vigilantes were all too eager to end.

It so happened, on September 18, that Keating was visiting Davis's ranch, and the two men had paused in their professional deliberations to take an afternoon siesta. They had unsaddled their horses and were bedded down beside them when a group of vigilantes came upon the pair. Whatever discussion ensued, the two rustlers were later found hanging from a tree. Spearfish Valley ranchers were delighted.

Charles Henry Borris

In 1875, Charles Henry, as his name was then, had been stealing livestock when he had the bad fortune to take some that belonged to the government. He went to the Wyoming territorial penitentiary outside of Laramie but managed to escape from the isolated facility and went back to the rustling trade.

But by 1878, using his full name of Charles Henry Borris, he'd blended stagecoach robbing with stock theft. He was in on the Whoopup Canyon robbery, and earlier in September he had been one of five men who descended on a stockraiser's camp in Wyoming. That group had taken fourteen fine horses—and everything else in the camp that was portable, right down to the wranglers' spurs.

Borris and Johnny Brown were arrested together in Deadwood. Like Brown, Borris said he hadn't participated in the Canyon Springs robbery. But Borris had a much better alibi to tell. He'd planned to be with that gang on September 26 but had taken some of the horses from the stock-raiser's camp into Deadwood to sell. Business accomplished, he used the proceeds to go on a spree in the saloons. And darned if someone didn't slip him a drugged drink that night!

He was passed out when the robbery happened. In fact, when he saw his robber pals after the robbery, he had to talk fast to convince them that he hadn't stayed away on purpose and betrayed them to the law.

Prosecutors got Borris on obstructing the mails. He was assessed a $100 fine but was ordered to stay in jail until he could pay it.

Charley Ross

Charley Ross, who did the shooting at the July 2, 1878, Whoopup Canyon robbery, sometimes went by the name of James Patrick, and some folks said they knew him as Jack Campbell.

He didn't stick around after the robbery and head to Deadwood with his pals, but lit out for Nevada. He landed in Eureka, a silver- and lead-mining camp just reaching its peak population. Since such camps attracted transient populations who moved around the same circuit, Ross shouldn't have been too surprised when someone recognized him. Cheyenne sheriff T. Jeff Carr traveled over to central Nevada and took Ross back for trial.

Ross was sentenced to a term of twelve years and sent to the prison at Lincoln, Nebraska, because the Wyoming territorial penitentiary was overloaded. There he contracted tuberculosis, which led to his suicide early in 1885.

THE MONITOR IS ROBBED AT CANYON SPRINGS
Bloody Victory over the Invincible Coach

On September 26, 1878, the invincible Monitor armored treasure coach was robbed. Unable to shoot through the reinforced walls, the bad boys realized that the way to get inside was to wait until the coach was stopped. They set up an ambush at Canyon Springs Stage Station, where the driver had to change teams. A large group of robbers was necessary for the venture, and afterward they split up and led five different posses on chases as far afield as Iowa. How many robbers were there and what happened to them all? No one really knows. Some conflicting tales have been pieced together to tell the story here and reveal the fates of some of the road agents.

H. Eugene "Gene" Barnett was driving the Monitor that day, with shotgun messenger Galen E. "Gale" Hill—a cousin of Boone May—beside him. Scott "Quick Shot" Davis and Eugene Smith rode inside, guarding the safe. Hugh Campbell was the only passenger, given permission to ride to Jenney Stockade, where he was being transferred by his employer, the Black Hills Telegraph Company.

After the coach left Deadwood, Andy "Red Cloud" Gouch stole a horse from a Deadwood lady of the night named Blanche White and galloped south to alert his compatriots that the Monitor was on its way.

At Canyon Springs Stage Station, efficient stock tender William Miner had been preparing for a routine seven-minute stop during which he would replace the tired horses with fresh ones. A man rode up on horseback and asked him for a drink of water, then drew down on Miner and shoved him into the stable's grain room. The robber was soon joined by at least four cohorts, and Miner heard them planning to rob the Monitor when it arrived. They made some gun holes by removing chinking between logs and got ready to fire from their hiding place.

When the Monitor arrived, and Barnett and Hill couldn't see Miner, Hill shouted out for him and then got off the coach to chock its back wheels. Rifle fire erupted from inside the log stable.

Far less elaborate than the stage line's Monitor coach but just as well armed, this "treasure wagon" and its well-groomed team carried out the fruits of George Hearst's Homestake Mine in Lead between 1876 and 1880. LIBRARY OF CONGRESS, #LC-USZ62-11769.

Hill was wounded in one arm but managed to hit one of the robbers. Then he took rifle fire to the chest—bullets passing through both his lungs—but either he or Davis hit another robber. The bleeding Hill managed to crawl to safety behind the stable, from where he wounded a third road agent before passing out from blood loss.

Inside the coach, one of the robbers' shots severely wounded Campbell and then grazed Smith's head. As the blood flowed, Davis thought Smith was dead; he survived though he was unconscious inside the stagecoach during the entire fight. Davis was firing as quickly as possible at the stable and got out of the coach to move behind a large tree that allowed him better aim. Despite his wound, the unarmed Campbell tried to move with Davis but was hit again and killed.

As Davis backed away from the coach toward the tree, firing constantly, he yelled at driver Barnett to come with him. But gang leader Charles Carey came out of hiding and went to the front of the team, captured Barnett, and used him as a shield against Davis. Carey yelled for Davis and his men to surrender, and Barnett pleaded, "For God's sake, Scott, don't shoot!"

According to Agnes Wright Spring, Davis then acted according to company policy that okayed abandoning the safe in order to escape alive. The safe, after all, was guaranteed to be break-proof once it was sealed. Davis ran seven miles to a ranch, where he borrowed a horse and rode on to Beaver Stage Station, ten miles south of Canyon Creek. There he found company shotgun messengers Jesse Brown, Billy Sample, and Boone May waiting to take over guarding the Monitor when it came in. They all galloped back to Canyon Springs.

Meanwhile, the robbers tied up their captives and told them someone would come at ten o'clock that night to release them. Then the road agents went to work on the safe, using a sledgehammer and chisel for two or more hours before they broke into it, grabbed the loot, and took off.

As soon as stock tender Miner could free himself, he ran to the Cold Spring Ranch Stage Station (the next one to the north) for a horse, then rushed on to Deadwood to raise the alarm.

Separate posses of lawmen and stage line employees spread out in all directions. W. M. Ward followed Duck Goodale all the way to Iowa. Deadwood sheriff John B. Manning headed into the Powder River country of northeastern Wyoming. Scott "Quick Shot" Davis first aimed west to Inyan Kara Mountain but later turned south toward Raw Hide Buttes. U.S. marshal Seth Bullock and shotgun messenger Boone May led a group riding east. At Rapid City, when this posse stopped to eat dinner, they picked up the sheriff, Frank Moulton, and other men.

Some men took the wounded Gale Hill to Cold Spring Ranch Stage Station, where a doctor came to treat him. After he recovered sufficiently, he was transported to the Deadwood hospital. It would be a full two years before the jagged bullet from his first wound pushed its way out of Hill's arm. But the wounds to his lungs shortened the man's life and impaired his ability to earn a living. Considered a local hero, he left the stage line and was given a job as deputy sheriff under John Manning, working off and on because of the permanent lung damage. Hill married in 1882 but died relatively young as a result of the Canyon Springs wounds.

Dogged trail riding and detective work, plus various robbers' confessions about where loot was buried, led to the recovery of three-fifths of the robbers' take within a few months. In hunting for the Canyon Springs robbers, lawmen rounded up many other road agents in that fall of 1878, making the road much safer.

Here are the road agents identified as Canyon Springs robbers and what we know of their fates:

Thomas Jefferson "Duck" Goodale

After young Duck (a childhood nickname) Goodale left his Iowa hometown in the spring of 1878, he wrote home, offering glowing accounts of how well he was doing as a Black Hills mine owner. It was the sort of success you might expect from the local farm implement dealer's son. (Local historian Doug Engebretson tracked down the information that Duck's father, Almond Goodale, was a farmer and implement dealer who kept a safe of his own in a local bank. That safe has caused authors over the years to assume that Almond was a banker.) Duck Goodale returned home in the fall and presented his father with a gold brick valued at $4,300. He asked his father to put it in his safe, explaining that he'd sold his share of the mine.

Then a Cheyenne and Black Hills Stage Company division agent, W. M. Ward, arrived in the little burg of Atlantic, Iowa, and announced that Duck had robbed the treasure coach called the Monitor. The young Goodale was found to have quite a few pieces of gold and diamond jewelry, including a lady's watch, among his possessions. The gold brick in his daddy's safe also had come right off the Monitor.

Agent Ward was eager to redeem himself because his boss, Luke Voorhees, had assigned him to ride the Monitor from Deadwood to Hat Creek Stage Station that day of September 26, 1878. Ward had gone only partway before returning to Deadwood. Then the stage was robbed, bloodily and spectacularly, at the Canyon Springs relay stop.

After the robbery, a posse led by Ward traveled to Pierre, Dakota Territory, where they got Duck Goodale's description. Alone, Ward followed Goodale's trail all the way to Iowa. He arrested the young man, who claimed that he and some others had stumbled upon the real robbers and stolen the loot from them. Ward got an extradition order, then had a railway blacksmith rivet shackles onto the robber's legs before they entrained, for the Hills, at Council Bluffs.

Near Lone Tree, Nebraska, Goodale asked to go to the washroom—and never returned. He had slid off his boots and the shackles and crawled out the window, possibly hiding atop the train until it stopped, and that was the end of his story. It was also the end of Ward's career with the Cheyenne and Black Hills Stage Company. Voorhees fired him as soon as he saw him.

William "Billy" Mansfield & Archie McLaughlin

Road agents William "Billy" Mansfield and Archie McLaughlin were busted in Deadwood on October 18, 1878, for trying to sell gold bullion to citizens upstanding enough to report them. They were taken to Cheyenne, but court wouldn't be meeting there for months, so back the law marched them, by stage, to Deadwood. Jim May (Boone's brother) and Jesse Brown, both stagecoach company employees, were guarding them.

Just past Fort Laramie, five masked men stopped the coach, disarmed May and Brown, and took charge of the prisoners. Placing nooses around their necks, they had the men climb atop the coach's roof. Mansfield cried and asked for time at least to write to his mother, but hard-case McLaughlin simply cursed his captors to the end. After finding a suitable tree, the masked vigilantes attached the nooses to it and drove the stage quickly away. Black Hills residents thought the vigilantes had done a public service, and no inquiries were made about their identities.

Al Spears

In Ogallala, Nebraska, M. F. Leach was both a shopkeeper and a deputy U.S. marshal. He learned that Al Spears—known in Deadwood as a cattle rustler and all-round bad boy—had sold $500 worth of jewelry and $800 in gold dust in Ogallala. He notified Luke Voorhees at the stagecoach company, then found Spears selling more stolen jewelry in Grand Island and arrested him.

Spears not only still had more pieces of jewelry from the Canyon Springs robbery on him, but he also was carrying Gale Hill's gun, taken during the same robbery.

In the end, Al Spears pleaded guilty to second-degree murder in the death of Hugh Campbell at Canyon Springs and was sentenced to life in the Lincoln, Nebraska, penitentiary.

Charles Carey

Early in October 1878, two men were found hanging from a tree near Jenney Stockade. People generally assumed that they were part of the Canyon Springs robbery crew and that Scott Davis's tracking party had taken care of them. Some people even claimed that one of the bodies was that of Charles Carey, none other than the gang's leader at the ripe age of twenty-seven.

Carey, they said, had been a scout for George A. Custer before turning to the criminal life. Records show, however, that he certainly was not working for the army as the 7th Cavalry moved toward the Little Bighorn River in 1876.

A miner named Frost, living in the Rochford area south of Deadwood, told the Black Hills Times that he'd seen Carey alive and well—after the robbery—traveling with Frank McBride and another man. They had stumbled onto Frost's cabin, where they were welcomed because Carey and Frost had once mined together. Frost had been amazed at how much gold they had, but he assumed it came from mining.

Whatever his fate, no one ever heard from Charles Carey again.

Frank McBride

The day after the Canyon Springs robbery, the combined posses of Seth Bullock, Boone May, and Rapid City sheriff Frank Moulton ran into a freighter who reported seeing a group of men on horseback traveling with a wagon that had a "sick" man lying in it. As the posses continued, various men had to turn back to Rapid City or Deadwood; Sheriff Moulton, for example, had to be in court the next day.

Those who were still traveling after dark suddenly heard horses somewhere nearby, but off the road. They stayed quiet and kept riding for a good distance before stopping to make a plan. May and Bullock urged attacking right then, in the dark, but they were outvoted. The winning argument was that the robbers had no idea the posse was onto them, and the posse members could surprise them at dawn.

When morning came, though, the posse found only the robbers' empty campsite and an abandoned wagon. They figured that McBride had died and been buried, so they rushed on in pursuit, but their only success was in picking up Andy Gouch.

On the return trip, one member of the Rapid City contingent, Dr. N. C. Whitfield, insisted on inspecting the campsite thoroughly, something no one had taken the time to do when they first passed it. He found an old pair of work overalls lying in the brush, checked them out, and discovered 650 ounces of gold. For that he earned himself a reward of $1,100 from the Cheyenne and Black Hills Stage Company.

Frank McBride never was seen in the Black Hills again. Maybe he lay in a hidden grave along the robbers' trail, or maybe he was the other man hanged near Jenney Stockade.

Andy "Red Cloud" Gouch

After the Canyon Springs robbery, the lookout who had ridden fast from Deadwood to alert the robbers made it all the way to Fort Thompson— on the east side of the Missouri River south of the Big Bend and north of today's Chamberlain, South Dakota—before he was arrested.

The robbery had been big news, and an alert deputy sheriff in Fort Thompson checked out the stranger who came to town, resulting in Gouch's capture. Confessing to his part in the crime, Gouch made it clear that he wasn't involved in the shoot-out and murder. He also cooperated with lawmen and stage line officials to locate part of the loot, some partially refined gold that had been stashed along the escape trail.

In return, Gouch was sent to prison only for his part in the theft, receiving a two-year sentence.

The Monitor's Fate

The Monitor continued its treasure runs until 1881, never being robbed a second time. The Black Hills gold rush's biggest years were 1877 and

1878, but after that the amount of treasure being sent out declined each year. In 1879, the Cheyenne and Black Hills Stage Company began running the Monitor on the cutoff to Sidney, Nebraska, where gold shipments were put on Union Pacific trains.

FRANK K. TOWLE
Beheaded by Boone May

Frank Towle (pronounced "toll") became more famous for what happened after his death than for the crimes he helped commit as a member of the Collins-Bass gang.

That Towle valued lawmen's lives but little was made clear in the final confession of "Big Nose" George Parrott in 1902. He recalled a time when he and Towle were in a gang trying to rob a Union Pacific train in Wyoming Territory in August 1878. They'd been camped and working to pry loose a rail so the train would wreck, but they not were having any luck because they hadn't brought a long enough crowbar. When they spotted two horsemen approaching, the bad boys hid in the brush.

The pair turned out to be railroad employee Henry "Tip" Vincent and Carbon County deputy sheriff Robert Widdowfield. The latter dismounted at the robbers' campsite and discovered that their fire was still warm, then shouted to Vincent that "we will catch them before long."

Frank Towle yelled out, "Let's fire!" and some men aimed at the squatting Widdowfield while others fired at Vincent, who was trying to escape on his horse. Both men were killed.

The month before, Towle had taken part in a robbery of U.S. mail from the stagecoach headed down to Cheyenne—or maybe in two robberies. The July 23 and 25 of 1878 robberies were the first times when the mail had been stolen, which historian Agnes Wright Spring attributes to the fact that the Monitor treasure coach was now in service. Robbers turned their attention to mail, hoping to find money or gold dust, even if in small quantities.

Postal detective John B. Furay, investigating in the area, said he had no doubt about the identities of the well-masked bandits, mentioning Towle as one of them, but regretfully admitted that he had no legal proof to take to court.

Late on the night of September 13, Frank Towle was with a gang who stopped the Deadwood-bound stage at Old Woman's Fork. They found only two passengers, a woman and a working man. After relieving the latter of only $10, the robbers returned it to him, took the mailbags, and let the coach go. They settled down to await the Cheyenne-bound coach and see what it had to offer.

Meanwhile, the Deadwood stage passed the Cheyenne coach, and its driver warned the other driver—and his shotgun messengers, Boone May and John Zimmerman—of robbers who might still be in the area. May and Zimmerman were riding horseback, not on the coach, and now they purposefully fell behind and out of sight.

Towle and the others stopped the Cheyenne stage, pulled off the mailbags, and began taking money and jewelry from individual passengers. Suddenly they discovered the approaching shotgun messengers and began firing at them. May and Zimmerman shot back, and Frank Towle fell. The other robbers yelled to the coach to go on as they retreated into a tight gulch and kept up their fire at May and Zimmerman. With no hope of rushing the robbers, the shotgun messengers left the scene with the stagecoach.

When lawmen returned in daylight, they found the mailbags left beside a pool of blood. Boone May claimed that he'd fired the shot that hit Frank Towle, but no one knew whether it had been fatal.

They found out three months later, after John Irwin had been sentenced to life in prison for his part in the Vincent-Widdowfield killings. He confessed that he'd been in on the September 13 robbery and that he and another robber had buried Frank Towle, and he gave directions to the grave.

By now, reward money was being offered for these murderous robbers, so Boone May found the grave, dug it up, and beheaded Towle's body. He carried the head to county commissioners in Cheyenne to claim his reward and also applied to the Carbon County commissioners at Rawlins, near where the murders occurred. But no one accepted that the grisly item May offered in a gunnysack was proof that he had dispatched Towle, so May went without the extra money.

WILLIAM "CURLY" GRIMES
Too Bad Even for the Horse Thieves

William Grimes seems to have been called "Lee" by some but "Curly" by many others. He was among the frontiersman who favored a long-haired look, wearing his blonde locks down to his shoulders. He also sported a mustache, which he sometimes dyed a darker color as a disguise. Some folks said he was the fastest shot west of the Missouri River, from the way he fanned his gun's hammer faster than its trigger would pull.

Curly Grimes had been robbing stages on the Deadwood-Cheyenne road for possibly a couple of years before joining a horse-rustling gang working south of the Black Hills. He and two other members, Jack Nolan and Joe Johnson, decided to rob the Bone Creek, Nebraska, post office. Since the horse thieves had been stealing Indian-owned horses, U.S. Department of Justice special agent W. H. Llewellyn was already on their trail. By stealing from Uncle Sam's post office on July 5, 1879, the smaller group caught the eye of U.S. postal inspector John B. Furay.

Warrants weren't issued for the postal robbers until October, mainly because the postmaster they had robbed believed their threat of death if he talked. His silence even made Furay think for a while that the scared fellow was in on the crime.

Meanwhile, James M. "Doc Middleton" Riley, head of the rustlers, had kicked Grimes out of his gang because he was too quick to shoot a man. Apparently Doc drew the line at murder.

After Nolan and Johnson were arrested, authorities learned that the third man in on the crime was Curly Grimes. By then he'd started working as a Black Hills freighter. Furay told Llewellyn to take Boone May with him for protection and track down Grimes.

They found the bad boy bullwhacking near Elk Creek south of Deadwood and easily arrested him while he ate dinner on February 3, 1880. With the mercury hovering around twenty below zero, Grimes pleaded with them to take off the steel handcuffs so that he didn't get frostbite, solemnly promising not to try an escape. By evening, in a thick blizzard, the trio was drawing close to Fort Meade at Rapid City, Llewellyn and May riding behind Grimes to cover him.

Suddenly, Grimes spurred his horse to get away, but the snow was too deep for him to make a break. Llewellyn and May both fired, killing Grimes. After making sure he was dead, they rode on into Fort Meade and reported the killing.

A burial detail was sent out from the post and the Deadwood coroner summoned. Many area residents began grumbling that Boone May was too eager to kill the sometime road agent and that Llewellyn was taking revenge on poor Curly Grimes because of his own failure to catch Doc Middleton. That led to a trial for the pair, who were easily acquitted of murder.

Grimes's grave remains where he fell, a mile east of the Black Hills National Cemetery in Sturgis.

HARRY LONGABAUGH
The Sundance Kid

Standing five feet nine inches tall, he was an inch above average height for a male in the United States. Although he had worked as a cowhand, he wasn't bowlegged, as the Pinkerton Detective Agency description noted (adding that he had small feet). He had brown eyes, light brown hair, and a round, full-cheeked face. He was twenty years old when first convicted of theft and jailed. From that incarceration came Harry Longabaugh's professional name: the Sundance Kid.

For much of his criminal career, he rode with the Wild Bunch, a loose confederation of small gangs and individuals who gathered together for large jobs, split apart to escape, and drifted together again. They weren't among the more violent robbers but were willing to shoot and traveled immense distances between jobs, showing up in the Black Hills, southern Wyoming, Colorado, and Nevada at various times.

From 1889 to 1901, the Sundance Kid moved around the West with the Wild Bunch. Then he and another gang member, Butch Cassidy, and Longabaugh's girlfriend, Etta Place, headed to South America. There they were honest ranchers for a few years, but then returned to robbing until the law caught up with them for the last time in 1908.

Harry Longabaugh was fifteen years old when he moved west with cousin George Longenbaugh and other relatives in 1882. (Still another branch of the family from Pennsylvania spelled their surname "Longbaugh.") The two young men worked as cowboys, and Harry made

Harvey "Sundance Kid" Longabaugh loved having his portrait made—for which Pinkerton agents were grateful as they searched for the Hole-in-the-Wall Gang. LIBRARY OF CONGRESS, #LC-USZ62-132506.

his way to Miles City, Montana Territory, in time to enjoy the hard winter of 1886–87, which decimated open-range cattle herds.

Longabaugh made his first trip to the Black Hills in early 1887, after being laid off in Montana, but found no work in the Dakota portion of the Hills. Late in February he was at Sundance, in the Wyoming Black Hills, when one cowboy's horse and saddle looked attractive, and so did another fellow's pistol. Longabaugh helped himself.

He was arrested in April and escaped, but he was green enough to return to Miles City, where he was known. In June, Crook County, Wyoming, sheriff James Ryan again picked up the thief. Longabaugh plea-bargained down three counts of grand larceny to one, for horse theft, and was sentenced to eighteen months in prison. He served the time in the Sundance jail. His one escape attempt failed, but a fellow prisoner with him got away.

Somehow, Longabaugh's attorney wangled a pardon from territorial governor Thomas Moonlight, but it came through only the day before his sentence ended, in February 1889.

The story goes that, celebrating his freedom, Longabaugh bragged to all and sundry about having served time in the Sundance jail—so much so that folks took to calling him the Sundance Kid.

By June of the same year, he was with Butch Cassidy, Matt Warner, and Tom McCarty when they robbed a bank in Telluride, Colorado. Even so, he went back to honest work on his cousin George's spread, then moved to Canada and worked on a ranch south of Calgary, where he bought an interest in the city's Grand Central Hotel. After the Sundance Kid was charged with cruelty to animals there, he returned to the States and hooked up with the Wild Bunch permanently.

Butch Cassidy, born Robert Leroy Parker, called his group the "Train Robbers Syndicate," but they rustled cattle, stole horses, and robbed banks and gambling halls as well as trains. They had an uncanny ability to split into small groups for escape, then reconvene at Hole-in-the-Wall (among other hiding places), in the rough canyon country of north-central Wyoming's Bighorn Mountains. There they could care for and slaughter stolen cattle; store greenbacks, gold, and jewelry for later use; and easily hold off approaching posses. Various wild women stayed with gang members in the hideout, providing all the comforts of home.

The group didn't have a sole leader or even a solid roster of members, but it collected members as needed for various jobs. Over his career, the Sundance Kid was not constantly in Cassidy's company.

The Wild Bunch weren't especially successful robbers at first. Sundance was living in Malta, Montana, when he partnered with Bert Madden and Harry Bass. They flagged down a Great Northern train outside of town and netted a total of $19.20—then naively returned to Malta. After they were captured, only Sundance escaped.

Belle Fourche (pronounced "foosh"), Dakota Territory, was the target for some of the Wild Bunch, including the Sundance Kid, on June 28, 1897. That day, neither the bad boys nor the townspeople could shoot straight (see more on this in the next story).

Next, Sundance and Harvey Logan and Walt Punteney came up with the bright idea of bribing a town marshal to leave town for a few days while they hit the local banks. They headed to Red Lodge, in the mountains north of Yellowstone National Park. Red Lodge was a rich little city, making its wealth from huge coal deposits and also serving as the shopping and service center for area cattle ranches.

To their amazement, the Red Lodge marshal turned down the business proposal, and the disappointed robbers left town. But a posse followed them and caught up in central Montana a few days later, in September 1897. Logan surrendered after being wounded in a gunfight, then Punteney and the Kid caved in, too.

They were taken to Billings, and Belle Fourche bank workers came to identify them as the robbers from the previous June. The three men were taken to Deadwood for trial, where the jail already held Tom O'Day, who'd been left behind in the Wild Bunch's haste to escape Belle Fourche.

The Sundance Kid petitioned the court for extra time to prepare their defense and prove their innocence, then the four Wild Bunch members escaped from Deadwood's jail on Halloween. O'Day and Punteney were quickly recaptured.

Now part of the Wild Bunch turned seriously to train robbery, hitting the Union Pacific in Wyoming in June 1899 and August 1900. After knocking over the First National Bank in Winnemucca, Nevada, in September 1900, the five men in this group had about $87,000 to split. They went to Fort Worth, Texas, to party—and made the great mistake of dressing up and having a studio portrait taken, all lined up in a row: Harry "The Sundance Kid" Longabaugh, Bill Carver, Ben "The Tall Texan" Kilpatrick, Harvey "Kid Curry" Logan, and Robert "Butch Cassidy" Parker.

The photographer was proud of his work and put it in a window to display his skills. A passing Pinkerton agent saw it, so the image soon graced wanted posters scattered around the West.

The Pinkerton Detective Agency, its logo the "eye that never sleeps," was more than thirty years old and had contracts with many railroad companies. Along with their clients, the Pinkertons were very interested in bringing down the Wild Bunch.

The Sundance Kid was now traveling with a woman who called herself Etta Place—not too coincidentally, Place being his mother's maiden name. The couple took their new riches to New Orleans and stayed through the New Year before heading to Pennsylvania. There she was introduced to the Longabaugh family as Mrs. Harry Longabaugh.

After that, they met Cassidy in New York. The couple signed into a rooming house as "Mr. and Mrs. Harry Place," with Cassidy as Mrs. Place's brother. Some of the train and bank takings went to Tiffany's, where the Sundance Kid bought Etta a fashionable lapel-pendant watch and treated himself to a diamond stickpin.

The next month, February 1902, the trio sailed to Buenos Aires, Argentina, where they deposited their money in a bank—one that they somehow considered safe. Cassidy stayed behind to purchase a ranch while the couple returned briefly to the States. During these months, the Sundance Kid and Etta had two mysterious hospital stays in New York State as well as two visits with the Longabaugh family. Some historians speculate that a sexually transmitted disease was affecting both Etta and Sundance.

Sundance and Etta returned to South America, and after three years of raising sheep, cattle, and horses, the trio apparently returned to robbery in both Argentina and Bolivia, with Etta holding horses and reloading guns. But not for long—she returned alone to the States in about 1905 and disappeared. The men sold their ranch and went to work in a Bolivian tin mine in 1907, where Cassidy became friends with a fellow worker who soon became the manager.

They didn't rob their own employer, but they did take the payroll from a nearby mine and also rode off with a mule that carried that mine's brand. Meanwhile, Pinkerton agents—free to travel internationally, unlike lawmen with set jurisdictions—had traced the group's path to South America and alerted local authorities of their presence. Two days after taking the payroll, on November 6, 1908, they were identified and surrounded in San Vicente, Bolivia, where both were seriously wounded in a gun battle. The Sundance Kid and Butch Cassidy chose suicide over being taken into custody.

THE WILD BUNCH FAILS IN BELLE FOURCHE
O'Day, Punteney & the Sundance Kid

The Butte County Bank in Belle Fourche was preparing to begin business bright and early Monday morning, June 28, 1897. Five customers, including a man of the cloth, waited inside as cashier Arthur Marble and the accountant, named Tinchnor, readied for the day.

The door banged open and four strangers rushed inside, shouting "Hold up your hands!" Then they seemed to freeze, not sure what to do next. So they ran from man to man, repeating the hands-up demand.

The robbers were Tom O'Day, Walter Punteney, Kid Curry, and "Frank Jones," the Sundance Kid's current alias. All were members of the loosely organized Wild Bunch.

Marble, a priggish-looking and well-fed young man, bravely snatched up a hidden revolver, but it misfired when he aimed at the robbers. Thus embarrassed, he too raised his hands.

The Reverend Mr. Clough, a Methodist minister, had been behind Marble, apparently using the bank's facilities to write a letter. He popped forward, claiming ecclesiastical poverty, but was roughly told, "Preacher be damned! Put up your hands." Clough escaped to safety inside the bank vault.

Across the street, hardware store owner Alanson Giles saw the raised arms above the bank's cafe-style curtains, and he foolishly ran across and opened the bank door. The sight of four armed men sent him scurrying back to his store, with one robber in pursuit. Down the street, a man named Tracy watched this and thought it was some type of prank.

After Giles ran through his own store and out the back to alert others,

Tom O'Day and Walter Punteney left the bank and began shooting up the street, including Giles's display windows. Kid Curry and the Sundance Kid followed, having managed to steal only $97 before the robbery went awry.

In the rush to escape, the Wild Bunch left O'Day behind, his horse running away with theirs. O'Day tried to steal a mule, but it would barely budge, and O'Day ran on down the street hunting for a horse to grab. He was captured before he did. In his pockets, townspeople found $392.50, so the town realized a net gain of $295.50 on this robbery.

Since the Belle Fourche jail had recently burned down, and some folks were talking about lynching O'Day, peace officers stashed him in the Butte County Bank's vault; they later transported him to Deadwood's intact jail.

Meanwhile, alert citizen Frank Bennett had climbed the grain elevator and begun firing at the escaping bandits. He shot and killed the horse of one robber who trailed behind the others—but this "robber" turned out to be blacksmith Joseph Miller, who was valiantly pursuing the real criminals.

A posse of maybe one hundred men took off after the robbers but never got within shooting range for the rest of the day. It was supposed that the trio escaped to Hole-in-the-Wall.

In September, Kid Curry, Walter Punteney, and the Sundance Kid went to and escaped from Red Lodge, Montana Territory, and were captured near Lavina in central Montana by the Red Lodge posse (see his previous story). Curry had other warrants, so he was handcuffed to his pals, and they eventually were taken to Deadwood for trial along with Tom O'Day. The Sundance Kid delayed the trial by filing a request for more time to prepare, and then all four escaped on Halloween. O'Day and Punteney were recaptured.

Punteney was tried first, charged with both the robbery and assault with a deadly weapon for firing his gun on Belle Fourche's main street. He was found not guilty of robbery, and his plea of self-defense on the gun charge was, amazingly, accepted. Even though he served no time, Walter Punteney left the Wild Bunch and went straight after this scare.

At O'Day's trial, Deadwood's jury tradition of going easy on the bad boys prevailed, and he was found not guilty. He hung out in town for a few days, accepting free drinks from low-class admirers before heading off to Hole-in-the-Wall. ⇥

CHAPTER FIVE

ENTERTAINMENTS
HIGH & LOW

THE GAME OF FARO

How They "Bucked the Tiger"

Faro, originally "pharaoh," was invented in France in the early eighteenth century. When Napoleon conquered Egypt and the nation was gaga over all things Egyptian, popular playing cards came with a pharaoh's portrait on the back and, voilà, pharaoh became the name of the game. In America, though, a common brand of playing cards was backed with a Bengal tiger, so "bucking the tiger" or "twisting the tiger's tail" were ways to describe playing faro in this nation.

Faro combined pure gambling and fast play, with players betting simply on what card would come up next. A faro set, or "bank," included a cloth or board printed with images of thirteen cards, ace through king, and a dealing box, a shoe to hold the used cards, and two types of tokens.

The dealer, called a banker, shuffled the deck and put it face up into the dealing box. After throwing away the first card, which players had seen, the dealer held the box and pulled out two cards per deal, the first being that deal's loser and the second its winner. Only the cards' values counted, not their suits. The single last card also was a throwaway.

Before the deal, a player put one type of token on a card's image (on the board) to bet it would go the player's way, or the other type to bet it would lose. He could bet on as many numbers as desired. Serious gamblers might bet ahead on a series of deals, creating all sorts of combinations.

Players didn't have to depend solely upon their memories. In honest games, the dealer used a "case keeper," which held domino-like images representing the values one through thirteen, with four abacus beads above each "card" that tracked how many of that rank had been played. A "lookout" also circulated around the table to guarantee honest dealing and honest betting.

Professional faro bankers owned their own layouts, traveling with them and setting up by arrangement in saloons and sporting houses. Many of these bankers were women, who sometimes used their charms to distract players and improve the bank's take. Two who turned up in Deadwood were Madam Mustache and, later on, Poker Alice Tubbs. Wyatt Earp and Doc Holliday also made their livings as faro bankers and were well known for running the game in their travels through the West. Earp carried his faro bank to Nome, Alaska, during the Klondike gold rush.

There was not much profit for the house in an honest faro game, and gamblers were likely to come out only about even in the long run.

CHUCK-A-LUCK
Fast, Furious & a Fool's Game

Gambling parlors and many saloons offered the chuck-a-luck dice game, also called "birdcage," which explains why "Birdcage Saloon" was a popular moniker for such businesses on the mining frontier.

The dealer put three dice into his birdcage, an hourglass-shaped wire container spun end-for-end with a crank. Players bet on whether a certain die, or combination of dice, would be thrown out after the spin.

Odds were very much against the players and for the house, the odds against calling a "triple"—three dice with the same number—being thirty to one. A miner could be shed of his gold dust poke in no time at all, but when someone won, he won big—and that kept them coming back.

NOT-SO-SOILED DOVES
Acrobats, Cancan Dancers & Dance Hall Girls
A woman could make a living being wild in various ways in the nineteenth-century Wild West and didn't necessarily have to be a prostitute. She could choose among several types of stage performing, all of which proper society still considered unrespectable.

In an era when a glimpse of stocking was something shocking and décolletage was only for formal evening wear, variety theaters drew male patrons with female acrobats. These women tumbled about the stage in abbreviated "Bloomer suits" and tights, showing off their forms as well as their gymnastic form—pretty "spicy" entertainment in the slang of the era.

Cancan girls danced in a style that waxed and waned in popularity in France throughout the 1800s, even being banned in 1830 by the French government as "revolutionary." Miles of frothy skirts and petticoats were vigorously flounced and waved about by a chorus line of cancan dancers performing high and low kicks guaranteed to reveal stockings, garters, and even silk underwear. It was another spicy act.

Hurdy-gurdy girls were dance partners for rent, called "dime-a-dance girls" in the early twentieth century. Their nineteenth-century name comes from a music box with small organ pipes; any unskilled operator could turn the crank and out came tunes produced from punched paper tapes that opened the pipes via pins. For small saloons and dance halls, it was a way to have some type of music, the variety among tunes depending solely on the house's investment in tapes.

A hurdy-gurdy house could be as small an operation as a husband-and-wife team—he the bartender and she the dancer. Large houses and dance halls might offer live musicians and a large selection of "girls."

Reporter James Chisholm of the *Chicago Tribune* characterized Cheyenne's dance houses in 1868 this way:

> *They are generally crowded to the door all night long, and*

the sound of fiddles and banjoes, mingles with the voice of the master of ceremonies. "Only two more gentlemen wanted for the next dance," as you hear it from the various halls, conveys the idea of a whole city being one huge rustic festival—an impression which is by no means sustained on entering the halls of mirth. A space in the centre is devoted to the terpsichorean art, where females of the lowest sort may be secured for the dance, while faro tables, keno, and all imaginable games constitute the side dishes.

Perhaps there were cribs in the back or upstairs, but dancing with a hurdy-gurdy girl didn't guarantee she was going to offer further favors. After the dance, her temporary swain purchased drinks, which were watered down and priced up, and the pair enjoyed a little conversation—not to mention a short rest for the working woman.

"HIT IT, PERFESSOR!"
The Hottest New Music
During Deadwood's heyday, "Professor" was a loosely used term of respect for any educated man, and it was always used for the solo pianist—or the ensemble conductor in a high-class brothel, larger dance hall, or top-notch saloon—even if frequently pronounced "Perfessor."

Every professor worth his salt had a full repertoire of works by the first American pop song composer, Stephen Foster, who flourished from the 1840s right up to his death in 1864. "Oh! Susanna" (1848) celebrated California's gold rushers, and so it remained a standard in all gold camps, combining goofy lyrics with grains of truth about the hardships that the listening prospectors had themselves experienced. "Camptown Races" (1850) was another fast, comic song that got the dance hall girls really "jigging," as any fast dancing was commonly called. More than one tough prospector may have dropped a tear or two into his beer over some of Foster's sentimental slow ballads: "Jeanie with the Light Brown Hair" (1854) or "Beautiful Dreamer" (1864).

At Jack Langrishe's performances of *Uncle Tom's Cabin* in the Deadwood Theatre, audiences might have enjoyed Foster's "My Old

Kentucky Home" (1853), often inserted into this melodrama as a musical interlude.

No doubt hurdy-gurdy tapes included plenty of Foster selections, familiar to listeners then although little known today. But Foster's work already fell into the golden oldies category by the time one could hear it in Deadwood.

A few of the then-new hits that some will recognize today are "Grandfather's Clock" (Henry Clay Work, 1876), "I'll Take You Home Again, Kathleen" (Thomas P. Westendorf, 1876), "Carry Me Back to Old Virginny" (James A. Bland, 1878), "Where Was Moses When the Lights Went Out" (composer unknown, arranged by Max Vernor, 1878), and "Funiculi Funicula" (Luigi Denza, 1880).

And then there's the classic "Oh! Dem Golden Slippers" (James A. Bland, 1879), which managed to be played in nearly every saloon scene in American movie and television westerns. Banged out quickly on a "rinky-tink"–tuned piano, it was guaranteed to get the girls' short skirts twitching and flying.

THE GEM & OTHER VARIETY THEATERS
Naughty Predecessors to Vaudeville

Deadwood's Gem Theater, Bella Union, and other variety theaters offered up-to-date entertainment for men of the Victorian era. Stage performances could include singers or poetry reciters specializing in double meanings, comedians, female acrobats, and cancan and other dancers—mostly women in abbreviated costumes.

Nationwide, many variety theaters (also called "concert saloons") featured "waiter girls" who wore skirts that reached only to their knees, shamelessly baring their calves to the world. Part of their job was to visit with patrons (including sitting on their laps) and encourage them to buy more drinks. In Deadwood, Nuttall and Brown's Temple of Music advertised, in late 1876, that its live musical entertainment was enhanced by "pretty waiter girls [serving]…the best Wines, Liquors and Cigars."

Deadwood's Bella Union was a success by September 1876, in terms of how many patronized it, but the *Black Hills Pioneer* noted that the vaudeville-type show was "a little naughty." Like the Gem and other

John Hanson Beadle's 1876 book, The Undeveloped West; or, Five Years in the Territories, *included this image of Deadwood's Bella Union Theater. Note the curtained cribs at left, where female staff entertained male customers.*
FROM J. H. BEADLE'S *THE UNDEVELOPED WEST,* UNIVERSITY OF MICHIGAN, MAKING OF AMERICA.

variety theaters, the Bella Union had curtained cribs around the stage, where some performers entertained paying customers in private.

Annie Tallent, one of Deadwood's earliest respectable women, characterized all the variety theaters as emphasizing "ribald song and smutty jest."

The typical program began with all the cast's ladies singing a song or maybe dancing a cancan, and then it went on through male comedians (ethnic humor was popular, with "Dutch" acts portraying uninformed German immigrants and "Irish" comedians portraying another large group of recent immigrants), "minstrel" acts, barbershop quartets, instrumentalists, trained animals, and the ever-popular acrobats in their tights. Minstrel comedians included both African Americans cracking jokes and singing in exaggerated Southern dialect and whites wearing blackface makeup. The latter became such a standard that later, in vaudeville, the popular African American comedian and singer Bert Williams had to don blackface in order to get gigs.

After a variety theater's acts came a comic sketch. These short plays became more complex in plot and music over the years and eventually helped lead to the American musical comedy. The variety acts took another path, toward vaudeville.

Reformers targeted variety theaters late in the nineteenth century, getting laws passed, in some states, that banned alcohol sales in theaters. After that, "family" and "high-class" became advertising code words for less-naughty performances.

As late as the 1890s, though, San Francisco's Belle Union theater advertised:

Full Grown People
Are Invited to Visit the
Belle Union
If You Want to Make a Night of It
The Show Is Not of the Kindergarten Class
But Just Your Size
If You Are Inclined to Be Frisky and Sporty
It's Rather Rapid, Spicy and Speedy
As Sharp as a Razor
And as Blunt at Times as the Back of an Axe

In such a variety theater, the waiter girls, singers, and other female performers were generally assumed to be available for after-hours entertainment as well—and almost all were. Many theaters included rooms for such entertaining or were surrounded by brothels and disreputable hotels.

Audiences at the Gem Theater themselves could be quite entertaining, too, with fistfights and other brouhahas breaking out until owner Al Swearingen's sturdy staff moved across the floor. Swearingen believed bashing heads to be quite appropriate for bringing order back into his lawless theater.

Ida Clark, who gave her occupation as "boarding house keeper" (often a code for "madam") to the 1880 U.S. Census agent, loved to attend shows at the Gem. But one spring night that year, the *Black Hills Times* reported, she was in a snit over something one of the dancers had said or done. She wrapped a shot glass inside her dainty handkerchief and slugged the other woman in the head. The dancer wasn't about to take that, and she was bigger (or at least stronger) than the pampered madam. When she retaliated, the audience was treated to a round of girl-on-girl fighting, and Clark went home worse for wear.

JACK LANGRISHE & COMPANY
"Father! Won't You Come Home?"

Jack (sometimes John) Langrishe and his wife, Jeannette, were well-established, fortyish stage performers when they brought their acting troupe to Deadwood in 1876, but sadly the records on them have many holes. They'd been presenting a mixture of Shakespeare and ever-popular melodramas since arriving in San Francisco during its gold rush days.

Whether ladies—and perhaps gentlemen—of the company (fewer than a dozen players) sometimes dallied with locals is not recorded. The Langrishes' goal, however, was performing on stage and not, like Al Swearingen, providing additional services. Regardless of how properly an actress of the day comported herself offstage, however, hers was considered a tainted, unrespectable occupation.

The Langrishe troupe offered *Hamlet* and *Othello*, but they also pleased crowds with the stage adaptation of *Uncle Tom's Cabin* and *The Drunkard; or Ten Nights in a Barroom*. The latter tearjerker, based on an 1854 pro-temperance short story, soon became a popular play around the United States, especially in small towns. Little Mary Morgan has come to the village tavern to retrieve her drunkard father, pleading "Father, won't you come home?" The evil barkeep throws a glass that hits the child on her head; after she lingers for a couple of days, the remorseful father promises never to drink alcohol again. Mary joyfully exclaims, "Oh, father! dear, dear father," just before she dies. And those are only the play's opening scenes. Further developments lead to the entire village going dry and preaching temperance to other towns.

Plays with such simple cause-and-effect plots, plenty of heavy emoting, and clear moral lessons were much to the taste of Victorian-era theatergoers—even in Deadwood, where most of the audience probably was drinking during the performance. And the Langrishe troupers made their livings by knowing and pleasing their audiences.

Actor Jack Langrishe dressed rakishly—perhaps in a character costume—for this undated studio portrait. DENVER PUBLIC LIBRARY, WESTERN HISTORY AND GENEALOGY COLLECTION X-19630.

In Deadwood, according to author/actor Thadd Turner, Langrishe leased and managed the Deadwood Theatre from James McDaniels, who also owned a successful theater in Cheyenne. Even though various memoirs refer to the building as the McDaniels Theater, Turner shows that its advertising never used that title. The Deadwood Theatre was also used for public meetings, court trials (it hosted most of Jack McCall's trial for killing Wild Bill Hickok but had to be cleared for the evening performance), weddings, and other large events. The theater began as a thirty- by one- hundred-foot arena with frame sides and a canvas roof, which one of the papers called a "mammoth pavilion theatre," indicating the soft top.

Beginning back in 1859, the Langrishe company had performed in theaters that Jack managed, and they also toured small towns, first based in St. Joseph, Missouri, and traveling through Missouri and Kansas. They landed in Denver in 1861, where they performed in the large Platte Valley Theater. The following year, Mike J. Dougherty bought the building, remodeled it, and opened it as the Denver Theater, under Langrishe's management. A saloon and gambling hall filled the first floor, with a large stage and seating for, it is said, a thousand people upstairs. (The theater was leased to someone else when it burned down in 1877.)

After Denver and at least one tour of Wisconsin towns, the Langrishes moved on to Helena, Montana Territory, in 1870, where they are credited with building the Langrishe Opera House, which went up in flames in 1874. After that loss, they apparently hit the road for a while until reaching Deadwood in 1876. First appearing and making a hit at the Bella Union, the Langrishes set up shop in McDaniels's new theater. After a couple of years, the Main Street location was too small, so a new one was built on Sherman Street, apparently called the Langrishe Opera House.

In Deadwood, theater parties soon became a stylish way for honorable couples to entertain, and local children were even allowed to play children's roles. Estelline Bennett tells of one smart lady who brought opera glasses to the tiny Langrishe theater, for the accessorized look rather than the looking. An old miner had to satirize such an affectation, so he inserted the bottoms of beer bottles into a board and soon showed up at the Langrishe with the contraption. Even the experienced Jeannette and Jack had trouble going on with the show when the old fellow's prank brought down the house—garnering laughter from its target as well.

Deadwood was home for the Langrishes until 1879, when the boom-town of Leadville, Colorado, beckoned, and the troupe moved there late in the summer. Once again, that September, fire took down a Langrishe-related theater when downtown Deadwood burned.

Both Langrishes acted in and managed the business of their company, and Jack is credited with writing occasional plays. He ended his days in Idaho, serving as a Coeur d'Alene justice of the peace and then as manager of the *Wardner News* in nearby Wardner. Jack's final curtain fell in 1895 in that town. Jeannette was still living there when the 1900 census was taken.

WORDS FOR WICKED WOMEN
From Frail Sister to Nymphs du Pavement

During Victorian times, the heyday of the Black Hills mining camps, middle- and upper-class women were discouraged from reading the newspapers because of the coarse and distasteful items they might see there. Stories of evil events would no doubt upset their delicate natures, which, as every man knew, were prone to hysterical problems anyway. Should the curious few (or those new-fangled agitators for the vote and the right to wear balloon-pants "Bloomer costumes" in public) sneak a peek, and lest the content offend men of refined sensibilities, newspapers carefully avoided many words. Family papers still do that today, but it's a different set of words.

One to be avoided was "prostitute," for which many synonyms were created, among them "daughter of joy," "daughter of sin," "soiled dove," "camp follower," "lady of the evening," "sporting woman," "nymph du pavement," "woman of the streets," "public woman," "notorious woman," "street walker," "fallen woman," "frail sister," and "Cyprian." Calling upon the reader's knowledge of the classics, the last referred to the island of Cyprus, legendary birthplace of the Greek goddess of love, Aphrodite. Historian Jerry Bryant refers to the *Black Hills Times'* frequent comments that Madam Mollie Johnston had welcomed a new group of "bankers' daughters" to her establishment.

Rather than working in "brothels," these women were said to put in their time in "disorderly houses," "sporting houses," "houses of ill repute," "maisons de joi," "bagnios," or "bordellos." But when the Black Hills camps experienced their first U.S. census, in 1880, these residences were classified as "boarding houses," run by "liquor dealers" or "proprietors" and occupied by women who gave their profession as "boarders" or, slightly more believably, "housekeepers."

"Madams" owned and managed the brothels, and some of them supported spouses or boyfriends, their "fancy men." These men were more likely lovers than pimps and were available as on-premises muscle when the clientele needed calming.

MONDAY AFTERNOONS FOR SHOPPING
Deadwood's Wild Women Have Their Turn

In earliest Deadwood, ninety percent of the female population worked as prostitutes. But, as the town developed, respectable wives and mothers joined their families there.

The proper ladies of Deadwood, by unspoken custom, avoided going to the downtown shops on Monday afternoons. That was when the nymphs du pavement had the freedom to replenish their sinful wardrobes with their ill-gotten gains—or at least what was left after they paid off their bosses. The merchants, of course, expected the "girls" to pay cash, because they were a very transient group.

Still, it was a small town, and faces were recognized. Should a wild woman be on the street downtown and meet a respectable but very liberal lady, a stiff nod of formal greeting might pass between them. Most gentlemen ignored prostitutes on the street—even if they might have known some of them rather well—but the tall, dignified, and universally respected Judge Granville Bennett chose to give the same polite greeting to any woman he passed, including those he recognized only from his courtroom. As he told some men who questioned the behavior, "I can afford to."

A DRINK ON THE HOUSE
The Bartender's Friend

When a guy was getting too rowdy in a sporting house, saloon, or gambling room, often the bartender would offer him a drink on the house if he would settle down. He could have some good whiskey, a little conversation, and both patron and barkeep would be happy. Maybe the dialogue went:

> *Barkeep: Hey, hey, we don't need any more holes in the ceiling. How 'bout you holster that gun and let me buy you a drink?*
>
> *Patron: Right neighborly—you know how to treat a man right.*

Then the bartender went about his mixologist duties while the whole room relaxed. But he added some chloral hydrate to his new pal's whiskey, and soon the brawler was off to slumberland. The term "Mickey Finn" for this special concoction didn't come into use until the early twentieth century, but bad boys (and wild women) in frontier saloons were well aware of what they called "drugged drinks."

In rougher places, the drink was used to prepare a man to be robbed while he was unconscious. Near the docks of San Francisco, a fellow could even awaken to find that he'd been sold into servitude on a clipper ship bound for Asia—"shanghaied," the sailors called it, after the city in China.

ACE MOYER, CON MOYER & "BIG STEVE" LONG
Saloon Owners Who Casually Robbed & Killed

At the Laramie City, Wyoming, saloon run by Ace and Con Moyer and Big Steve Long, who were half-brothers, they didn't waste time on the subtlety of a drugged drink. They simply bashed in a man's head and put out his body for the wolves to eat. Whether they saw their saloon as a cover for robbery and murder, or whether they considered this just a lucrative sideline, no one knows.

The Moyers and Long built their saloon at Laramie City when the town was first laid out in 1868 to serve as the newest Union Pacific terminus. Many Cheyenne residents, to the east, were relieved that "hell on wheels" had moved on down the rails.

The new saloon was soon a headquarters for the transient populace of railroad construction men. If they noticed that some of their fellow workers didn't come back to camp after a night's celebration there, they probably thought nothing of it. Fellows were always joining and leaving the crews.

Bootless at his own request, Big Steve Long was hanged beside his Moyer half-brothers by Laramie, Wyoming, vigilantes in 1868. WYOMING AMERICAN HERITAGE CENTER.

Laramie City's more respectable residents, though, began to notice. Big Steve Long had gotten himself appointed deputy marshal, and his brothers volunteered their saloon's back room as a temporary court and detention facility. But so many men went into that room and never came out that some locals soon were calling the establishment the "Bucket o' Blood."

As a lawman, Long had an unfortunate record of frequently having to kill someone he was trying to arrest—he said they just kept drawing on him and forcing him to defend himself.

It seems that the three brothers also began bullying area ranchers, trying to get them to turn over property deeds to them. All things considered, the ranchers organized a vigilance committee. One of their leaders was Nathaniel K. Boswell, who had been running a Cheyenne drug store, had been the first county sheriff, and was appointed a deputy U.S. marshal; when Wyoming's territorial prison opened in 1869, he would serve as its first warden.

The vigilantes seized the three cold-blooded brothers in late October 1868, then hanged them together from the rafters of a cabin under construction. Long had just one request—that the vigilantes remove his boots. He wanted to prove his mother's prediction wrong: She'd always said he'd die with his boots on—that is, violently.

ADOLPH CUNY & JULES COFFEY
Adding a Brothel: Purely a Business Decision

The businessmen who owned Three Mile Stage Station near Fort Laramie didn't set out to be brothel owners, but they added this amenity to their considerable spread when the government forced them to. Well, in a way.

Adolph Cuny and Jules Coffey built the stage station on the Black Hills Trail in 1873, as traffic to and from the Hills began picking up. They already ran 2,000 head of cattle and 150 horses on their ranch and had been trading with both the U.S. Army and the Sioux for years. This stage station was one of the road's most elaborate, with a large store, blacksmith shop, and ice house. A billiard hall welcomed soldiers from the fort, and Fort Laramie's quartermaster regularly hired teams and wagons from these merchants.

But the year after the station opened, the government attempted to drive prospectors out of the Hills. Men who had flocked to Cheyenne to go north and try their luck stayed in Cheyenne, and stage traffic dropped tremendously. The soldiers were still at the nearby fort, though, so Cuny and Coffey now built eight two-room cabins for occupation by Cyprians. They hired their first ten women by spreading the word in Omaha, Kansas City, and other frontier hubs. Calamity Jane was one of their early crib residents.

Women at the lower-class houses like this one often wore soldiers' uniforms, obtained from their swains or from cooperative post tailors. A woman wearing pants in public was scandalous all by itself, regardless of how she made her living. Having uniform clothing also came in handy when a wild woman wanted to stroll into Fort Laramie and mingle with her pals on the parade ground or join a military expedition—a ruse Calamity Jane was fond of using.

Adolph Cuny had come a long way to start his little empire, emigrating from the Burgundy region of France with two brothers when he was eighteen, back in 1849. One brother went to California, the other to Chicago, but Adolph went to Canada and got into the Indian trade. He moved south to Fort Laramie, where he married Josephine Bissonette in 1860.

Josephine was the daughter of French Canadian trader Joseph Bissonette and his first wife, an Oglala Sioux named Julie Hubert, herself possibly of French Canadian heritage. Adolph and Josephine became the parents of four children, a son and three daughters, between 1862 and 1870. They kept close ties with Josephine's relatives at Pine Ridge on the Great Sioux Reservation, and she often visited home.

Adolph's business partner, Jules Coffey, had been living and trading with the Sioux in the Fort Laramie area. He was born of French Canadian and possibly Indian heritage. His name seems to have been Ecoffe, but he Americanized the spelling to Coffey. Bissonette was friends with Chief Red Cloud and went as a translator with the Sioux delegation to Washington, D.C., in 1875, when the U.S. government sought to buy the Black Hills.

In 1876, Three Mile Stage Station held a big blowout to celebrate the United States' one-hundredth Fourth of July. Coffey went to Fort Laramie ahead of time, asking to borrow an artillery piece to put some real oomph into the proceedings; he was turned down, because the fort would be using all their guns for their own celebration. When the summer of 1877 rolled around and the Black Hills rush was on, the Cuny and Coffey businesses were doing quite well indeed.

Late in June, the news came around that the Cheyenne-bound stage had been stopped and robbed three nights in a row, at the Cheyenne River crossing. About four days later, Josephine Cuny set out on horseback to visit relatives at Pine Ridge. Adolph was at the Three Mile Stage Station when Fort Laramie's deputy sheriff, Charles Hays, rode in and said he had word that the robbers were near, at the Six Mile Stage Station. Adolph Cuny and one of his employees agreed to be deputized and go along to help arrest them.

Riding the road to Pine Ridge, Josephine Cuny heard voices urging her to return to her husband, as the story has been passed down among her descendents. She headed back to Three Mile.

At Six Mile, Hays arrested two of the robbers—Clark Pelton and Dunc Blackburn—then left Adolph Cuny to guard them while he and the other temporary deputy searched the premises for more robbers. Pelton must have had a hidden gun, because he shot and killed Cuny. He and Blackburn temporarily escaped custody, but eventually Pelton would be sentenced for manslaughter in Cuny's death.

Josephine Cuny was waiting at Three Mile when news of her husband's death came. Soon after, she soon packed up her children and moved home to Pine Ridge to raise them alone, living to the age of one hundred and four (she died in 1936). Cuny Table in the South Dakota Badlands carries that name through her son Charles, and some of Adolph and Josephine's descendents still ranch in the area.

For Cuny and Coffey, getting into the brothel business had been purely a business decision, not indicative of their way of life.

PORTER'S HOTEL
Home Away from Home for the Dance Hall Girls
Porter's Hotel was one of the few in Deadwood that welcomed dance hall girls and their ilk, so it became the residence of choice for many of them. Calamity Jane stayed there during her early days in the mining camp.

Porter's was managed by William Lull, a fresh-faced youth whom most people called "Billie," and some called "Baby-Face." A Methodist minister's son from New York, he didn't smoke, drink, gamble, or otherwise carry on—but he also didn't appear to judge his wild patrons. Residents of the Badlands entertainment district enjoyed teasing Lull about how good he looked as a result of all that clean living, but he just laughed and took it in stride. He was, after all, having the adventure of a lifetime.

AL SWEARINGEN
Slave Master on the Frontier

Records of the life of Ellis Alfred Swearingen are sparse. (His name is often spelled Swearengen, but collateral descendents spell it with the middle "i.") An unsigned article by Jerry Bryant in the Adams House Museum's *Adams Banner* newsletter states that Swearingen and his twin brother, Lemuel, were born in Iowa in 1845, the eldest of eight children. Al was gone from there by the time the 1870 census was taken.

He came to the Black Hills early in the gold rush and, according to Sam Young, built his own saloon in Custer City in 1875. The log building had a wooden floor, with sleeping quarters for dance hall girls in the back and a separate kitchen/dining room shack where the women cooked and ate. In addition to liquor, Swearingen offered gambling, with eight professionals on staff, and dancing with a choice of fourteen women.

When the gold prospectors moved on to Deadwood in 1876, Swearingen and his first wife, Nettie, went with them. Upon his arrival in May that year, he erected a wooden-floored saloon dance hall in a canvas tent and hired Calamity Jane and Kitty Austin (also called Arnold) as dancers. According to some, Kitty was Swearingen's wife at the time—at least his second one, because he had already been divorced once since arriving in the Hills. In all, three wives would divorce him, each claiming physical abuse and infidelity. Estelline Bennett regularly saw a Swearingen wife in the early 1880s displaying a blackened eye and sometimes limping down the street.

From Deadwood, Swearingen began his practice of advertising, especially in small-town Iowa and Nebraska newspapers, positions for young ladies as respectable family or hotel servants. He also traveled to Chicago

In this view of the Gem Variety Theater's bar, Al Swearingen is seated right of center.
BLACK HILLS MINING MUSEUM.

to recruit young women and used Calamity Jane as a hiring agent at least once. Some who answered were younger teens, and some were recent immigrants with little command of English. When his new hirees arrived in Deadwood, they discovered what work the boss actually had in mind: prostitution. Few had money to turn around and head home, and no doubt many were ashamed to have been deluded, so they stayed and worked.

Swearingen kept the women in virtual slavery, likely through the same method many madams used: The women had to give about half their income to the house and then pay for their food, lodging, clothing, doctor visits, and other services. This system worked like that of southern sharecroppers of the era, with the employee always in debt and never quite able to work off what was due. Swearingen abused and intimidated them physically and mentally and ordered the same from his general manager, Dan Dority, and his "box herder," or manager of the girls, Johnny Burns.

Besides recruiting through the newspapers, Swearingen at least once outfitted Calamity Jane with a team, wagon, and camping supplies. She traveled as his agent to Sidney, Nebraska, and brought back ten recruits.

Swearingen is also said to have run a small saloon, the Cricket, where in late 1876 he sponsored a not-uncommon entertainment of the day: a bare-knuckle boxing match. In a tiny ring, refereed by another saloon owner, two miners fought to a draw—after fifty-two rounds. To show how acceptable an event like this was, a newspaper favorably reported the excitement, and a later bare-knuckle bout even featured the town marshal as a boxer.

In April 1877, Swearingen opened his Gem Variety Theater on the Cricket's former site, having built an edifice that included a properly curtained stage, dance hall, saloon, and gambling parlor. It soon was Deadwood's premier house of entertainment for men. Late the following year, though, a judgment against Swearingen for nonpayment of debts gives a glimpse of how he handled business. The judge put the Gem on the auction block, but no one bid against the bad-tempered Swearingen, and he bought his theater back.

Swearingen was charged with assault and battery many times and likely committed it even more often. When his patrons got too rowdy even for Swearingen's liberal tastes, they were not only kicked out but also beat up. Records show that Swearingen was also charged with non-payment of taxes at various times.

The Gem burned down, along with all of downtown Deadwood, in September 1879. Assessed at $6,000, it was one of the town's most valuable buildings lost in that fire. Its quickly built replacement burned the next month. Then Swearingen erected a grander, larger, two-story Gem, so obviously business was still good.

His shows followed the usual variety theater format, with comics, musicians, singers, dancers (male and female, solos and groups), minstrels, and novelty acts, with a house orchestra to accompany them. These "novelty acts," in theater terminology, indicated trained animals, skaters, trapeze artists, child actors, and local Sioux Indians re-creating traditional dances. Swearingen regularly imported performers and even hired a traveling talent scout to recruit new acts for the Gem.

Curtained cribs around the stage provided facilities for prostitution, and Swearingen expected all of his female employees to take customers into them upon request. Needless to say, respectable ladies and families did not attend the Gem, no matter what headliner was appearing on its stage.

Adjoining the theater was a new and improved Gem Dance Hall, complete with an orchestra whose music carried merrily out into the street.

It has been estimated that, at the Gem's height of popularity, Swearingen was taking in something like $35,000 during its seven-day week—in an era when a factory clerk made $18 for a six-day work week and a salaried silver miner $24, according to national census statistics.

By the 1890s, Deadwood was no longer a boomtown, but it retained its status as an area service, shopping, and entertainment center. The population, estimated at 10,000 during the height of the gold rush in the late 1870s, was now fewer than 3,000 souls. In 1892, Deadwood's Methodists tried to have the Gem shut down, but apparently the business's status as a local draw still protected it. Miners by then were employed in corporation-owned hardrock facilities rather than working for themselves.

All the same, Swearingen was deeply in debt, and his saloon closed when the Gem burned down once again in 1899, the victim of arson. He left the Black Hills and, five years later, died destitute. ⊸

CHAPTER SIX

FRAIL SISTERS
OF THE
FRONTIER

CATS FOR THE HOUSES
Frontier Supply & Demand

This event was recorded, as an afterthought, in Deadwood newspapers, but its retellings have altered enough that one can trust only the basic details. Still, it's a perfect example of boomtown entrepreneurs, and of the law of supply and demand prevailing on the mining frontier.

Apparently, in 1877, a male employee of one of the bordellos went to the *Pioneer* newspaper office to place an ad. The saloon and its upstairs rooms had a mouse problem, which was putting off patrons and upsetting the girls. Management had decided to buy a dozen cats, and surely an ad would bring forth felines for purchase.

A reporter pointed out that there were no cats in Deadwood, coyotes having gotten the very few that pilgrims had brought to town—and very few gold rushers bothered traveling with pets.

Somehow the bordello employee connected with a man, likely a freighter already heading to another town, who agreed to bring back cats for the house, at $10 apiece. Possibly his trip took him all the way to Cheyenne, where he paid small boys twenty-five cents apiece to capture animals for him. He returned to Deadwood with more than the required dozen—maybe seven or so times that number—delivered the contracted dozen, and collected the agreed fee.

Then he parked his freight wagon at a downtown intersection and offered the remaining cats for $25 to $50 apiece, quickly selling out the entire stock at an enormous profit.

Some have said this was the origin of the term "cathouse" for a brothel, but a look into a large dictionary quickly disproves that connection, since it leads one back to fifteenth-century English usage.

At any rate, Deadwood now had a check on its rodent population, and the working girls had some pets to pamper. But things didn't work out so well for all of the cats, as research by historian Jerry Bryant has revealed.

When that first cat shipment arrived, Ed Reilly bought one of the felines, a male he named Patsy, for only a few dollars because it had been "sea-sick" (according to the newspaper) throughout the wagon trip from Cheyenne. Patsy regained his health and turned out to be an excellent mouser—his owner's pride. When Deadwood burned in 1879, Reilly had to rescue Patsy from his house, but time and again the cat "struggled, bit, scratched and twisted until he got loose and ran back into the building." To Reilly's great sadness, Patsy didn't survive the fire. The newspaper thoughtfully added, "The Latin maxim, 'rest cat in peace' comes in here," punning on the Latin "requiescat in pacem," which is abbreviated R.I.P. on tombstones.

Other cats had escaped their owners and turned feral, with "an army" of them raising Cain near one man's cabin for several nights. When he went to investigate, he found them "howling, fighting and screaming" over a partially eaten human arm. The gentleman "beat a hasty retreat," the newspaper reported, and decided he could put up with the noise.

And then there were actor Jack Langrishe's cats, which chose to live under the *Black Hills Times* newspaper offices, a couple of doors down the street from Langrishe's theater. The editor begged in print, "Col.

Langrishe, please come and take your cats from under our office. They will kill each other fighting if you don't look after them." A witty writer then turned to poetry to make the complaint humorously:

> **Another Cat Fight**
> **Dedicated to Col. Langrishe**
> Your cat and another climbed upon our roof,
> > In the clear, cold frost last night;
> And there, beneath the silent moon,
>
> > They fought a furious fight.
> They madly fought for two full hours,
> > A fierce contested match;
> Each in his pur-puss firmly fixed,
>
> > To come up to the scratch.
> At last one howled, "I feline need
> > Some rest, so let us paws,
> And in our sanguinary code
>
> > Insert a friendly claws.
> They ceased, and crouching on that roof
> > They sounded their cat-arrhs,
> And sang in tones that rent the air.
> > The mews[-]sick of their wars.

GEORGIA DOW
Lucky to Get Away

No. 10 Saloon bartender Sam Young recalled, in his sometimes untrustworthy autobiography, Georgia Dow, a woman he called the "queen of the dance hall girls in Custer." Young said he had known her previously in Hays City, Kansas, making this author wonder whether she had been his love there, on whom he'd spent all his money one long night—earning himself some sage advice from Wild Bill Hickok.

Young saw Dow again in Custer City in late 1875 or early 1876, when she arrived among a group of fourteen "girls" brought to the Black

Hills by Al Swearingen. For them, Swearingen built a dance hall, a log building with a wooden floor, with fourteen small rooms at the back to serve as the girls' quarters. Behind the dance hall, a shed held kitchen and dining facilities exclusively for the girls' use.

Dow stayed in the Hills until autumn 1876, continuing to work in the dance hall. Then she moved south to Sidney, Nebraska, where Young heard that she "partially" reformed. Noting that she lived to the then-estimable age of sixty, Young commented:

> This is very remarkable, as that class of girls dissipated awfully and were frightfully abused by their lovers, who took from them all they could earn and frequently punished them severely when they did not earn enough.

Georgia Dow was lucky—or wise—to get away from Al Swearingen in such a short time. Many dance hall and brothel owners treated their employees badly, but Swearingen seems to have been among the worst of the worst.

MARTHA "CALAMITY JANE" CANNARY
Captured by Her Legend

Near the end of 1879, just three years after she first arrived there, Calamity Jane left Deadwood claiming that it had become "too puritanical" for her tastes.

Deadwood was becoming more settled, but it didn't take very much for any place to be too pure for the low tastes of Martha Jane Cannary. From her teens, she was an alcoholic who made a hand-to-mouth living mainly as a dance hall girl, prostitute, and camp follower with the frontier army and railroad construction crews.

Drunk most of the time, she was always getting into scrapes and fights and having accidents—just one calamity after another. Historian James McLaird, author of the definitive Calamity Jane biography, explains: Newspaper headlines of the era frequently used the word "calamity," for example, calling the San Francisco earthquake and fire the "San Francisco Calamity." Hard-luck men were "Calamity Joe" and hard-luck women "Calamity Jane" in more than one location. But Ms. Cannary became *the* Calamity Jane when dime novelists used the nickname, and she began depending on the legend for her own survival.

No one knows whether she actually came to believe the tall tales of the dime novels, but Martha Jane certainly enjoyed telling them for free drinks or lecturing in a dime museum. Having seen the inside of a schoolhouse for only a few months of her childhood, she spoke poorly, but she peddled a ghostwritten "autobiographical" pamphlet, along with pictures of herself, in her last years. The legend, at least, supported her.

Martha Jane Cannary was born in 1856, the first child of a farmer and his much younger wife, who herself was a rowdy, foul-mouthed, illiterate woman he may have met in a bawdy house. The family joined the gold rush to Montana country in 1864 and lived in Virginia City and Alder Gulch for a while. That December, the children were neglected and hungry when Martha took it upon herself to get help. She carried her infant sister Lana, and led little brother Cilus, to knock on the door of upstanding citizen James Fergus and ask for help. Mrs. Fergus and a neighbor scared up some food and clothing for the youngsters, and someone carried the news to the local paper. Its outraged article labeled the children's father a gambler in nearby Nevada City and their mother "of the lowest sort."

Before the children's mother died in 1866, one more brother, Lige (Elijah), was born. The surviving family moved to Salt Lake City, where the father died the following year, when Martha was eleven. Not much is known about what happened to the other children at that point— although in her later life she was in touch with her siblings Lana and Lige—but by her mid-teens, Calamity Jane was supporting herself by touring the railroad-building camps and military forts along the Union Pacific Railroad in Wyoming Territory.

She was not considered beautiful, her long face surrounded with dark brown hair (some said dark auburn) and illuminated by piercing eyes called "steel blue" and "blue-gray." Her liveliness, fearlessness, and inveterate pranking set her apart from other prostitutes much more than her looks did.

The raucous railroad camps were home to hardworking men doing dangerous labor and living away from their wives and families. A camp would be set up at the end of the laid rails. Trains delivered construction and other supplies while the men laid track beyond their location to a point where a new camp was opened. When a newspaperman named such moving camps "hell on wheels," the phrase became part of American slang.

Calamity Jane may have started out as a hurdy-gurdy girl, or dancing partner, but soon she was working as a prostitute. In 1873, at the age of seventeen, she was among ten Cyprians employed at the Coffey and Cuny road ranch, Three Mile Stage Station, on the Black Hills Trail.

The following year, she later claimed, Calamity Jane met up with George A. Custer at Wyoming's Fort Russell, then went with him to Arizona to fight Indians. But Custer never was at Fort Russell or in Arizona. George Crook had fought Indians in Arizona, and possibly the wrong "General George" ended up in her autobiographical pamphlet. And Calamity Jane never made it to Arizona, one way or another.

Working at Coffey and Cuny's ranch put her near Fort Laramie, and soon she was among the regularly visiting prostitutes who wore soldiers' clothing in order to blend into the crowd more easily. When troops traveled with General Crook to the Black Hills in 1875 to remove prospectors, she went along—but in no official army capacity.

Many writers have accepted Calamity Jane's claim that she worked as a bullwhacker in the Black Hills and Wyoming area. Biographer McLaird, who spent ten years researching her hectic life, found no proof of that, although he acknowledged that she sometimes traveled with freighters. He did discover one Mrs. Oleson, the only "female bullwhackeress," as a Deadwood paper labeled her in an 1886 article. Perhaps that woman's adventures were appropriated for Calamity Jane's spurious autobiography.

Calamity Jane went along, too, at the beginning of Crook's expedition against the Sioux, which culminated in the Battle of the Rosebud, Montana Territory, on June 17, 1876—an Indian victory that boosted Sioux and Cheyenne confidence one week later when Custer attacked them on the Little Big Horn River. But she wasn't present for the actual Battle of the Rosebud. General Crook, early on his northward trip, had discovered her and other prostitutes among his troops and sent them back with his supply wagons to Fort Fetterman in Wyoming Territory.

Her later claims to have scouted for him (or any other army officer) are also false—Crook always preferred using local Indians as scouts.

She made her way south to Fort Laramie, where celebrating the soldiers' payday left her drunk and half-clothed in the guardhouse. Just then, late in June 1876, a train of Black Hillers organized by Wild Bill Hickok and Colorado Charlie Utter arrived. The captain of the guard suggested he release Calamity Jane to their custody, and they agreed, putting together men's buckskin clothing for her to wear. She promptly attached herself to Charlie's brother Steve for the duration of the trip, and others in the party would have laughed if they heard her claim in later years that she and Hickok had been planning their wedding when he was killed.

Joseph "White Eye" Anderson (so named because a flying cinder during a prairie fire had turned one of his eyebrows white) was also in the Hickok-Utter party. He noted that it was the first time Hickok had met Calamity Jane, and that the dapper gunman "surely did not have any use for her." The pair's main contact was when Jane asked for access to Hickok's whiskey supply, saying she was "dry" again—so often that Hickok told her to slow down and leave some for the others.

As would happen for the rest of her life, Calamity Jane was thought to be older than she actually was. Now twenty, she'd always had a rough life, and White Eye credited her with twenty-five years. In the future, the discrepancy between her actual and perceived ages would only increase—ultimately to three decades. White Eye also recorded that she drew nightly crowds around the campfire by telling "some of the toughest stories I ever heard."

More than a dozen other prostitutes and madams had joined the train, including Kitty Austin (Arnold), Madam Mustache, and Dirty Emma. When the Hickok-Utter train paused at Custer City, this "crew of depraved women" did not impress the local newspaper. The party soon moved on to Deadwood.

They made quite an entrance, too, with Calamity Jane, Wild Bill Hickok, and Colorado Charlie riding down the street in their buckskins—the two men sporting long curls and the woman just as unusual with short, "bobbed" hair long before it was stylish. News blazed through camp that a whole wagonload of women had arrived.

Calamity Jane stayed in Deadwood while Hickok, the Utter brothers, and Anderson made camp at claims in the Engleside area (later absorbed into Deadwood).

Before she could get to work, though, she had to put the arm on the boys, asking for a loan for clothing because "I ain't got the show the other girls have" in the buckskin suit. (It should be noted that her eternal idea of a "loan" was a one-way transfer of funds, to herself.) White Eye Anderson said that Hickok gave her $20 and the advice to wash behind the ears. Hickok, who had the unusual habit, for the time and place, of taking an entire bath every single day, had probably been itching to give her that advice ever since Fort Laramie.

In her new finery, Calamity Jane was soon working for Al Swearingen as a dance hall girl and staying drunk most of the time. Deadwood bartender Sam Young, who had known her previously, said she once went to Sidney, Nebraska, and brought back ten new women to work for Swearingen.

Fewer than three weeks after his arrival, Hickok was dead; twenty-six years later, Calamity Jane claimed that he and she were soon to be wed, but that was her "dime novel" self speaking.

The first dime novel with the "Calamity Jane" character came out in 1877 and succeeded so well that it led to a lengthy series featuring her as partner of "Deadwood Dick." The fictional woman was skilled at every frontier art, fearless, sober, and honest to a fault, frequently contracting with the U.S. Army as a scout. The real-life woman was said to be capable of hitting five bull's-eyes out of eight shots at one hundred paces, but that is about the only overlap. There is no record that she ever worked in any capacity for the army—her only association being as a camp follower.

Calamity Jane roamed around the Black Hills area and beyond—Sturgis, Rapid City, and down to the Hat Creek stage ranch and Cheyenne—over the next five years. She seemed unable to stay in any single place for long, possibly being invited to leave when people tired of her raucous ways. In a saloon, she slapped every "Dearie" and "Darling" (all her best friends, whose names she never seemed to remember) on the shoulders, occasionally shot the place up as a hilarious prank, cadged drinks and "loans," swore fluently and loudly, and fought with both women and men—one of her moves being a high kick landing square on the chin. A Deadwood paper claimed, though, in February 1879, that "she never fights unless she is in the right, and then she is not backward to tackle even a masculine shoulder hitter."

She also regularly announced her "marriage" to the latest man she'd taken up with. There was a practical reason for this besides a sad reach for respectable social status: It was a jailing offense for a man and woman to live together without the benefit of clergy in those days.

When Calamity Jane was living with a man and caring for his ranch house or freight camp, she had a respite from making her own way, even though she never had a partner who treated her to a better life. After interviewing her in the 1880s, a Cheyenne paper concluded: "Heart and affection were to her unknown terms, and when the revenue failed so did the lover." Cowhand Wirt Newcom of Miles City, Montana, recalled her saying, "I never had a fellow with a hell of a lot of money; I always did pick a good-looker."

After her first Black Hills years, Calamity Jane went back to following railroad construction camps in western Dakota Territory and across Montana Territory. A mining rush to the Idaho panhandle attracted her in the mid-1880s, but not for long. She saw brief employment in a Wild West show that toured from Wisconsin to Chicago, where a drunken shooting binge in the street by its cowboys was the last straw for the financially strapped owner. After that show foundered, Calamity Jane lived in Wyoming until about 1894.

Her sister Lana, now calling herself Lena, and brother Lige (by now an ex-con) also lived there. As Calamity Jane passed from her twenties into her thirties, she may have run a laundry with her sister, but she also made money traveling to the "hell on wheels" railroad construction camps in Wyoming and western Nebraska.

When she was thirty-one, Calamity Jane gave birth to a daughter, Jessie, whose father is unknown, as is detailed information about who raised the child. Historian James McLaird believes the father to be Bill Steers, described by a Lander, Wyoming, newspaper as "slightly built, sickly looking, and unassuming." He beat Calamity Jane (who fought back but occasionally called for help from the law) severely enough to land in jail. Still, they married in Pocatello, Idaho Territory, in 1888, seven months after Jessie's birth—and then split up permanently.

When Calamity Jane met Clinton Burke and began living with him in a tent on an Ekalaka, Montana, cattle ranch, she had Jessie with her. She and Burke never married, but she claimed they had (in El Paso, Texas, where she'd never been) and used his name for the rest of her life. They were together off and on from 1894 to 1896.

In October 1895, Calamity Jane took Jessie to Deadwood, where she hoped to enroll her in a convent school. She later told an interviewer that she wanted Jessie educated, "so when I do go she will have some way to support herself if she don't get married. I never had no chance to learn nothin'. I don't care what they say 'bout me, but I want my daughter to be honest an' respectable."

But the Deadwood classmates teased Jessie so mercilessly about her wild mother that Calamity Jane moved her to St. Martin's Academy in Sturgis after a few weeks. The mother needed a place to leave Jessie while she made her second stab at show business.

Before she left, the old pals from Deadwood held a benefit for Jessie's Sturgis tuition, choosing the ultra-notorious Green Front Theatre in the Badlands district, a favorite hangout for Calamity Jane and many of her friends. Handed the money, the wild woman proceeded to treat everyone to drinks, beginning a week-long spree for her, according to madam Dora DuFran. The toot ended with Calamity Jane literally passed out in the street, her feet washed in waste water running down the gutter. DuFran took her home to sober up, and a friendship began.

Charles Kohl and George Middleton, who ran dime museums in the Midwest, hired Calamity Jane, and husband Clinton Burke, too, at the beginning of 1896. They would appear in Minneapolis, Chicago, Philadelphia, New York, and other cities, where her billing was

> *The Famous Woman Scout of the Wild West*
> *Comrade of Buffalo Bill and Wild Bill*
> *Terror of Evildoers in the Black Hills*
> *See This Famous Woman and Hear Her Graphic*
> *Description of Her Daring Exploits!*

Now the dime novel heroine had become the real-life Calamity Jane's way of making a living.

Dime museums were combinations of freak shows ("curiosities of nature"), exhibitions of skill, and lectures by the famous and infamous. Their aspirations to respectability dictated that speakers neither swear nor use slang, surely a stumbling block for the foul-mouthed Calamity Jane. She memorized a ghostwritten script telling the alleged story of her life and gave shooting demonstrations. From then on, this tale was what she told reporters, starting from the beginning and reciting it straight through without being stopped.

After the tour, and until the end of her days, she made her living mostly by selling the dime museum's "autobiographical" pamphlet—that script—for fifteen cents a copy, plus postcards holding her picture. Sometimes amenable merchants allowed her to trade the items for groceries. In 1897, Calamity Jane was issued Special Permit No. 1 as a vender in Yellowstone National Park, in order to sell her paper goods, and she would make summer trips there for several years.

Her dime museum tour lasted until the end of May 1896, when she returned to Deadwood, reclaimed Jessie, and moved first to Wyoming Territory and then to Montana Territory. Clinton Burke, who had left the show after its second stop, rejoined her in Deadwood but soon returned to Montana without his wife and never lived with her again.

The last record of Jessie's being with her mother comes from 1898 when, according to a classmate of Jessie's, mother and daughter were living in an old house in the Billings, Montana, factory district. A California woman named Jessie Oakes, according to historian McLaird, wrote to western states' historical societies in the 1930s asking about her "grandmother," Calamity Jane, and remembered living in Billings with her. Ms. Oakes said that her grandmother's "last husband" took the girl away from her when she was about ten years old.

In the late 1890s, Calamity Jane moved around even more than before. She sometimes worked as a laundress, she failed as a cook, and she also partied in railroad camps where spur lines were being built in South Dakota, Wyoming, and Montana. She sold her pamphlets and photos and could be loud, vulgar, and pushy to passing pedestrians who weren't interested—leading to regular police invitations to move on to the next town. Sometimes she wore a buckskin tunic and pants, as represented on one of the postcards, and often she wore shabby dresses.

She ended up in jail more than once, delirious from her drinking or its sudden stop.

By 1901 some of her teeth were missing and her face was deeply lined. People assumed she was at least ten years older than her forty-five years. Despite the heavy drinking, she still accepted another show biz offer and traveled east. It didn't go at all well, with Calamity Jane jailed for drunkenness in upstate New York after receiving her first paycheck. She made her way to the city of Buffalo, where Buffalo Bill's Wild West show was appearing, and Bill Cody bought her a ticket to return home and gave her $25 for meals on the trip. She ran out of money in Chicago and worked in dime museums there and in Minneapolis to put together a stake. When she continued the train trip, she sold pamphlets and photographs en route but also stopped off for sprees in several South Dakota towns.

Bouncing around Montana, in and out of jail, she now was often ill enough that people got her medical attention in addition to helping her sober up, however briefly.

Calamity Jane returned to the Black Hills for the last time in mid-summer of 1903. Deadwood photographer John B. Mayo talked her into going to Wild Bill Hickok's grave to pose for a photograph. He said she was "woozy, panting, and weaving as she plodded along" up the steep hill, and then fell asleep standing while he focused his camera.

She soon traveled to Terry, South Dakota, a few miles away, where she was so ill from what was politely called "inflammation of the bowels" that residents put her into a hotel and summoned a doctor. After lingering a week, Calamity Jane died on August 1. The local paper stated that she was seventy-three, but her age actually was forty-seven.

The Terry newspaper editor arranged for her burial in Deadwood with funds from the Society of Black Hills Pioneers—open only to those who, like Calamity Jane, had been in the Hills during the first two years of the rush. One member said the Pioneers thought it was a good joke on Wild Bill Hickok to bury her near him, and so it was done; after all, when Hickok was safely dead, Calamity Jane had begun claiming that they were a couple. A Deadwood paper claimed that the burial site was at her request, starting another enduring myth about her.

Calamity Jane had lived the rough life of the Old West prostitute, living hand to mouth most of the time and using drink to deaden the pain. Her dime novel fame and sojourns into show business led to a life of enough celebrity that we can follow it through newspaper articles over the years. Unlike Calamity Jane, most women who lived as she did experienced their sad lives in anonymity.

KITTY AUSTIN (ARNOLD)
Set Up with Her Own Parlor House
Kitty Austin, also called Kitty Arnold, arrived in Deadwood in the summer of 1876 in the Hickok-Utter caravan, and her beauty elevated her to the top ranks of the train's twenty Cyprians when the miners greeted them.

According to Calamity Jane biographer James McLaird, Kitty and Jane at once went to work in the brand-new, small dance hall of Al Swearingen, who later built the Gem Theater.

Kitty soon ran her own parlor house, or high-class brothel. Calamity Jane, never a beauty, wasn't invited to work there, so sometimes when Jane was in her cups, she'd swing by Kitty's place and fire a few bullets at it.

LITTLE FRANK
Calamity Jane's Drinking Buddy
The petite Little Frank, or Shingle-Headed Frank (meaning she must have worn her hair bobbed, as Calamity Jane often did), or Soldier Frank, was one of Jane's pals for drinking and pranking around Cheyenne. Her last name has been recorded variously as O'Day and O'Dare, and her first also as Frankie. The two Cyprians went on benders together, sometimes renting a buggy from a livery stable for a tour, and just as often upsetting it by wild driving and daring, drunken tricks.

Little Frank and Calamity Jane both donned their soldier clothing and joined troops leaving Fort Fetterman at the beginning of the Great Sioux War, in March 1876. But General George Crook soon discovered them traveling amid his command and sent them back to Fetterman with his supply wagons.

Besides being a prostitute, Little Frank had her own faro bank. She now put it to good use among the relatively few, bored troops who had remained to man Fort Fetterman. Then she and Calamity Jane took the proceeds to Cheyenne and went on a spree.

MOLLIE JOHNSON
Queen of the Blondes

The sparse facts known about Mollie Johnson, who flourished in Deadwood until about 1881, suggest that she could have been a proto-type for the "madam with a heart of gold" so beloved in books and films. She was generous to local charities, staunchly supported Irish famine relief, and required her "girls" to speak properly and behave as much like ladies as they could.

She was also flamboyant, enjoyed flaunting her presence in town, and knew how to give great parties. Her regular, for-profit "grand balls" were always well attended and were said to be a great place for tenderfeet to make new friends. Johnson and her three girls were blondes—whether or not they were born that way—and hers was as much a high-class house as any in Deadwood.

Johnson was well known for renting an expensive carriage and being driven around town, flaunting herself to the proper ladies and pointedly snubbing the prostitutes not refined or beautiful enough to work for her. She and her girls once rented two rigs to go to Fort Meade, at Sturgis, and take in a baseball game. They imbibed freely while there and, on the way home, decided that a buggy race between Crook City and Deadwood was in order. Of course, their inexperience as drivers, combined with drunkenness, led to a grand crash. Only one girl was injured, and she was helped by passersby. Upon that woman's arrival in Deadwood, gallant rescuers rushed out to collect the rest of the blondes.

Mollie Johnson told the census taker in 1880 that she had been born in Alabama in 1853, the daughter of Irish immigrants, and that she was widowed. How and why she came to Deadwood as a madam remains unknown.

In February 1878, she married Lew Spencer, a popular musical come-dian in the town's variety theaters, where he performed a minstrel act in blackface makeup. Some accounts therefore have confused him with Len (short for Leonard) Spencer, a nationally known African American minstrel who made the first recording of "A Hot Time in the Old Town" in 1897, but Len was only eleven years old (and living in the East) when Mollie Johnson married Lew.

Marriage didn't change Mollie or her profession, and it seems to have had little effect on Lew as well. The year after their wedding, he took a solo trip to visit friends in Denver. Deadwood was surprised to read in the papers that, while there, he shot and killed his wife. Not Mollie, obviously, but another one. Lew went to prison, and that was the last known about Madam Johnson's supposed second husband.

Did she care for her girls? One story hints that she either sincerely did or could make a great show of it. Mollie Johnson's house, near the corner of Sherman and Lee streets in Deadwood's Badlands district, was unfortunately near the Empire Bakery—source of the great fire of 1879. As her house was burning, a distraught Johnson screamed at the few firefighters that she couldn't leave until she knew that her girl Jennie was safely rescued.

It turned out that Jennie, née Josephine Phillips, had died after a brief illness—possibly caused by a cat bite on her face. She was laid out in the parlor when the fire started, and Johnson refused to be consoled until the casket was retrieved from the flames.

The blondes' home was a complete loss, but like the rest of Deadwood's businesspeople, Johnson immediately rebuilt and went back to work. Her destroyed facilities were valued at twice that of many other stores and business buildings.

When Deadwood's placer gold played out, Mollie Johnson apparently joined the exodus for greener pastures, disappearing from the historical record—at least, under that name.

MADAM MUSTACHE
Faro Dealer & Madam

Eleanor Dumont was a charming young woman when she followed the gold rush to California, blessed with flirtatious dark eyes and a winning personality. She was welcomed as a faro dealer and for many years made a good living at it. She also soon was a madam.

Dumont claimed to be Parisian by birth, but perhaps she was only born of French immigrant parents. Still, among the frontier's entertainers and soiled doves, European ancestry imparted both mystery and class.

Some say she was called Minnie the Gambler at first. Then, what is always referred to as "downy hair" on her upper lip gave Dumont the nickname Madam Mustache, by which she continues to be known.

In the later 1850s, Dumont flourished in Nevada City, California, where her gambling house was said to sport crystal chandeliers and free champagne. Guests had to scrape the outdoors off their boots before striding onto its fine carpets.

She was said to have a temper, one she put to good use in taking care of herself. One night when she left the gambling tables a winner, two thieves attacked her in the street. She killed one and wounded the other.

When the northern California boom ebbed, Dumont moved on to the Comstock rush in Nevada, and from there on to wherever the next big strike came, including Idaho and Montana. The building of the Union Pacific Railroad across the United States drew her to Cheyenne to prey on the construction camps. From there, the natural next stop was Deadwood Gulch, so she and her girls joined the Hickok-Utter train in 1876.

Dumont opened a house in Gayville nearly as soon as the town existed, in 1875. By then she was middle-aged, and some say her sharpness at the faro bank was no longer what it had been. Sometimes she had to turn tricks on the side to make ends meet.

As Deadwood's surface gold declined, Dumont moved on to Tombstone, and then back to California, settling in Bodie, fifty miles south of Lake Tahoe. One night in the fall of 1879, her fortunes were so low that she had to borrow $300 from a friend to make the evening's faro play. Two male cardsharps beat her every hand, cleaning her out financially. After leaving the tables, Dumont committed suicide by consuming a bottle of morphine.

CHARLOTTE SHEPHERD
Mother Featherlegs

Charlotte Shepherd had a mass of red hair and favored old-fashioned lacy pantalettes that ruffled in the breeze as she rode astride her horse. After some wit said, "Them drawers looked exactly like a feather-legged chicken in a high wind," Shepherd became known to one and all as "Mother Featherlegs."

Her brothel opened along the Black Hills Trail near the Raw Hide Buttes Stage Station (south of present Lusk, Wyoming) in 1876. She offered gambling, bad whiskey, and prostitutes, but she had another business, too, the one that got her killed.

Mother Featherlegs welcomed road agents, other robbers, and rustlers to her establishment. Besides sharing whatever law enforcement news came her way from passing traffic, she held stolen goods temporarily when thieves wanted a safe place to stash them. No doubt she earned a share of the booty in the process.

After she'd been in business for about a year, Dick Davis moved in with her. He claimed to be a professional hunter and trapper, but he never seemed to be absent from the brothel. People observed that the couple knew each other well, but no one knew where either had come from. And, on the western frontier, that was not the kind of question to ask.

Davis had an evil and sneaky look about him, so those who met him in the West took to calling him "Dangerous Dick."

Later researchers traced the pair back to the swamps of northern Louisiana, where Shepherd, known as "Ma'am," and her sons Tom and Bill were part of a gang that included Davis, called "The Terrapin" back there. During and after the Civil War, they robbed and killed travelers, then retreated to a watery hideout. When vigilantes swept down and hanged the boys and other gang members, Charlotte and Dick escaped.

Back in Dakota Territory, one day in 1879, a respectable homestead lady decided to ride overland to call on her sole female neighbor, Mother Featherlegs. She arrived to find her dead, shot while filling a bucket at the spring by her dugout. Dangerous Dick was gone, and so were any money and valuables that might have been inside the house.

Davis went back home to Louisiana and took up his land piracy where he'd left off. When he was captured, he was hanged near where the Shepherd boys had been, years before.

Before the hanging, he confessed to being part of the old swamp pirates gang and to killing Mother Featherlegs for her riches.

Her story doesn't end with her burial, though. She'd been at rest near the dugout for a while when Russell Thorp, Jr.—son of the Cheyenne and Black Hills Stage Line's final owner—and a pal decided to open the grave. As he recorded:

> [We] camped nearby and proceeded to do this job at night. It was a beautiful moonlight night. This was, as I recall, about the summer of 1893—14 years after her death. When we removed the lid of this homemade pine coffin, her features were clearly recognizable, with a great mass of red hair. We hastily nailed the lid back down. After all those years the body had more the appearance of being slightly mummified, and the coffin was not rotted.

Russell Thorp, Jr. (1877–1967), who first learned to drive a stage from legendary driver George Lathrop, grew up to become a prominent cattleman in Wyoming and Montana. He spent a lifetime preserving stagecoaches and their equipment, forming the collection now exhibited in the Stagecoach Museum of Lusk, Wyoming.

When a Cheyenne-to-Black Hills stagecoach run was re-created in 1964, Thorp and his treasures were part of the action. Even more appropriate, one of the festivities was dedicating a 3,500-pound pink granite marker at Mother Featherlegs's grave—and Thorp unveiled it. The stone declares:

> Here lies Mother Featherlegs. So called, as in her ruffled pantalettes she looked like a feather-legged chicken in a high wind. She was a roadhouse ma'am. An outlaw confederate, she was murdered by "Dangerous Dick Davis the Terrapin" in 1879.

Some claim this to be the United States' only monument to a prostitute, but in this era of cultural tourism, that seems unlikely.

PEARL LEOPOLD
"I'm Done For"
Pearl Leopold was buried on Valentine's Day 1884, in Deadwood's Mount Moriah Cemetery, amid floral tributes and "arrayed in a costly dress." Her casket was silver-plated and bore a silver plaque that stated

she was "At Rest." The officiating minister used this occasion to offer a lesson to her sister soiled doves on the dangers of their line of work.

Leopold had worked at Rose Barnett's brothel in Deadwood until, in January 1883, she left for the greener pastures of Spearfish. There, brothels served the rough "cowboy element" employed on area ranches, but the houses were much less welcome than in Deadwood.

Working from the Murray House in Spearfish, Leopold had somehow infuriated a cowboy named Fred Higgins. On February 12, 1884, she was climbing the stairs to the second floor when Higgins and another cowboy, William Hill, arrived and shouted for her to come down. Higgins pistol-whipped Leopold, breaking her nose. Then he emptied his revolver into her.

When he stopped shooting, he called out to her, and she replied that she was "done for." But Higgins wasn't satisfied. He pulled her upstairs by the hair and undressed her sufficiently to check the wounds. Satisfied that she was going to die, he and his partner left the house.

They soon left the Black Hills country as well, after putting out the word that they wouldn't be taken alive—implying that they'd do their best to take some lawmen with them.

Leopold's body was returned to former employer Barnett's house on Wall Street in Deadwood, from which the well-attended funeral was held.

Upright Spearfish residents were appalled at the "ruffianism" that had occurred in their midst, even if it did happen to a frail sister.

FANNIE HILL
A Madam in Lead's Tenderloin

Fannie Hill was a successful madam whose houses served miners in Lead for going on twelve years starting in 1897. Beginning with four girls, she eventually employed eleven in her maison de joi. She seems to have graduated from soiled dove status herself, being well known in Lead's tenderloin district before she opened the house. To explain her single status, the lady claimed to be a widow, at the tender age of twenty-nine.

No one knows her real name. Perhaps she took her professional one from the 1750 erotic novel, published in England, called *Fanny Hill; or, The Memoirs of a Woman of Pleasure*. Author John Cleland and his publisher were charged with "corrupting the King's subjects" back then, and in 1963 the U.S. publisher G. P. Putnam's Sons fought Massachusetts's banning of its new edition. (The U.S. Supreme Court overturned that ban three years later, saying the book did not meet the standards of obscenity.) The novel shocked readers with its graphic sexual content, but even more so because Hill enjoyed her work way too much and never reformed.

Hill of Lead ran a generally discreet house, but one night in the summer of 1905, police responded to a monstrous fight between her and one of her employees. The two women had screamed curses, bitten, scratched, punched, pulled hair, and torn off much of each other's clothing by the time they were arrested. A doctor was summoned to the jail to attend to Hill's black eye, but the working girl seems to have gotten the worst of it. Hill had left deep scratch marks on her face and bitten out flesh from her chin.

Hill stayed in business for at least four more years, though, faithfully paying the monthly fine that was the cost of doing business in Lead's tenderloin. Where she went after that—and what name she used—is not known.

DORA DUFRAN
A Lifelong Madam

Amy Bolshow was born in England in 1874 or 1875, just as the Black Hills gold rush began, growing up in Nebraska after her family emigrated to the United States. How she found her way to the Hills, and whether she was ever a prostitute herself, doesn't seem to have been recorded. But, as Dora DuFran, she successfully ran brothels in Belle Fourche, Deadwood, and Rapid City during a long career as a madam.

It seems that her marriage to the gentleman gambler twelve years her senior, Joseph DuFran, gave Dora great support in both life and work. They met when she was operating a sporting house in Deadwood. He definitely accepted her chosen field, and they seem to have had a fine relationship until his death at age forty-seven, in 1909. Dora buried him in Deadwood's Mount Moriah Cemetery.

During her Deadwood days, Dora was known for contributing generously to charitable drives, offering a place for the ailing to stay, and quietly helping out the downtrodden.

She is credited with having owned four brothels during her career,

In her surviving studio portrait, madam Dora DuFran seems every bit the jolly English girl she was born. ADAMS MUSEUM AND HOUSE, INC., DEADWOOD, SOUTH DAKOTA.

but the name of only one seems to have been recorded. (One reminiscence, however, claims she owned Deadwood's ultra-sleazy Green Front Theatre in 1878, but she would have been three or four years old then.) Beginning around 1900, early in DuFran's career, she owned Diddlin' Dora's in Belle Fourche, which she advertised as

Three D's
Dining, Drinking and Dancing—
A Place Where You Can Bring Your Mother

Well, maybe to the downstairs saloon—depending on what your mother was like—but upstairs were rooms for the prostitutes and their clients. During Calamity Jane's last year of life, DuFran hired her as an occasional maid and cook, made sure she ate, and tried to keep her away from the bottle. In 1903, when Calamity Jane went on her final bender, she left from Diddlin' Dora's.

After Calamity Jane's death, DuFran published a pamphlet combining Jane's biography as told to her and her own knowledge of the last days. In it the madam moralized: "It is easy for a woman to be good who has been brought up with every protection from the evils of the world and with good associates."

Sometime after DuFran's husband died, she owned a Rapid City bordello that apparently attracted the city's prominent businessmen. One night, Rapid Creek favored the town with one of its frequent flash floods, which stranded a notable number of these elite gentlemen in DuFran's establishment. By the time the waters receded and they could make it home, word had passed among the men's wives as to just where they'd sheltered during the flood.

Like Poker Alice Tubbs, Dora DuFran was welcome to participate in Deadwood's Days of '76 parade, and she enjoyed doing so beginning in the 1920s.

In her later years, DuFran was famous for being the gentle owner of a pet parrot named Fred. The bird is buried in the DuFran family plot, where Dora joined Joseph in 1934. On her grave, four urns decorated with beaming little devils are said to memorialize her four brothels. ⚬

CHAPTER SEVEN

MORE WILD WOMEN

LURLINE MONTE VERDE
Nurse—or Manager?—for a Robber Gang

By the time she arrived in Deadwood in 1876, the widow was using the name Lurline Monte Verde and supporting herself as a card dealer. According to Agnes Wright Spring, Monte Verde sometimes performed as a "serio-comic singer" at the Bella Union theater and saloon. She also dealt poker and danced a jig from time to time. Later she opened what she called a "restaurant," which was likely a saloon and gambling room. This became a hangout for some stage robbers. To relax, Monte Verde enjoying visiting Deadwood's Chinatown and floating away on clouds of opium.

Monte Verde must have talked to the boys in the restaurant about her marriage to a doctor, claiming that he had taught her some skills of his trade. She did tell that story to a Cheyenne newspaper reporter in 1878,

This image of an unidentified but high-class dance hall (note live musicians rather than a hurdy-gurdy machine) portrays workers and a spectrum of clients.
DENVER PUBLIC LIBRARY, WESTERN HISTORY COLLECTION F-6269.

adding that after her husband's death she had briefly taught school on the Great Sioux Reservation before turning to card dealing to support herself.

At any rate, in mid-July 1878, robber Billy Mansfield briefly came by the restaurant and told her a friend of his was seriously ill and needed help. Monte Verde was to meet Mansfield at an opium house they both knew that night, and he would take her to the friend.

Mansfield led her to a small house where she met Archie McLaughlin and another man, who also insisted their friend was merely sick before administering "a solemn oath of secrecy" about their identities and the situation. Then they conducted her to what seemed a "deserted shanty...not too far distant." She recognized the "sick friend" as Johnny H. Brown.

Monte Verde realized that these bad boys were among those being sought for a stage robbery on July 2, by then ten days ago (although she would claim later that Billy Mansfield was innocent). They were hiding out in the woods by day and spending nights at the shanty.

Brown was in bad shape, coughing up blood and pus and suffering from a high fever with delirium. He was convinced his companions were trying to kill him, oblivious to the risk Mansfield and McLaughlin had just taken to bring help. Monte Verde calmed him down with a chloro-form-soaked cloth, examined him, and discovered a bullet between two ribs on his right side.

She later told the Cheyenne reporter that the bullet had gone through his liver before lodging at the ribs, where she inserted a wire loop to pull the bullet out. Brown's only assistance for enduring the pain was doses of chloroform.

After the operation, Monte Verde went to the shack daily to tend her patient. On the next night, two more gang members (Charley Ross and Charles Henry Borris) were hiding under Brown's bed to monitor her conversation. Monte Verde pretended not to have seen them and changed the dressing.

She saved Johnny Brown's life, but he soon was captured. Some said that the handsome Boone May wormed his way into Monte Verde's affection and got her to identify the robbers. By the time Monte Verde talked to the Cheyenne reporter, some of the robbers had been lynched, others arrested, and Brown himself had confessed to lawmen. She maintained that Billy Mansfield wasn't one of the robbers and had been lynched unfairly. Still, he was clearly involved in the gang and with the robbery's aftermath.

After the *Cheyenne Leader* published what the woman may have thought to be a deathbed confession, national newspapers and the thirty-three-year-old tabloid *Police Gazette* played up the tale of the frontier "woman physician" serving outlaws.

Historian Agnes Wright Spring mentions that some people claimed Monte Verde had been a spy during the Civil War, before which she'd grown up in comfort in Jefferson City, Missouri. Other names she had supposedly used were Belle Siddons, Madam Vestal, and her married name of Belle Hallet.

In 2006, Dustin D. Floyd, writing for *Deadwood Magazine*, stated that Belle Siddons had grown up on a plantation near Jefferson City and attended college in Lexington, Kentucky, before the war broke out. In fact, that city did have a women's school founded in 1854, Sayre College, and no other women's college opened there until 1869. Belle Siddons served as a spy for the Confederate side, then drifted west as a card dealer.

In Deadwood, under the name of Lurline Monte Verde, she collected information at the gaming tables and in her restaurant to pass on to her lover, gang leader Archie McLaughlin. Some say that she, an educated woman, was actually the gang's planner as well, organizing and scheduling their robberies. After vigilantes hanged McLaughlin, she tried to commit suicide.

As Deadwood's fortunes declined, Monte Verde moved on to other western boomtowns to make her living. She died in San Francisco around 1880—in an opium den.

HENRICO LIVINGSTONE
The Terror of Small Children

In the late 1870s, "Miss" Henrico Livingstone lived alone in a rough little Deadwood cabin near City Creek, working her mining claim out back. She sometimes hired additional male workers and frequently dressed in men's clothing while she dug.

Her obituary would state that she was *Mrs.* Livingstone, and that she had enlisted as a man in the Union army during the Civil War, then fought alongside her husband through most of the war.

According to Estelline Bennett, a child in the 1870s, Livingstone cut a "tall grim figure, shabby, stiff, and dour." She was ever ready to protect her honor, and her claim, with her trusty Winchester.

She also made money as a "Medical Clairvoyant" and fortune teller, under the name of Madame Henrico, inviting clients with her newspaper advertisement headed "Know Thy Destiny."

Unfortunately for Livingstone, the schoolyard abutted her property and, from time to time, children crossed the invisible line onto it. Happily, she didn't use the rifle to get rid of them, but she would throw stones at the young claim jumpers. The children, recognizing a good competition when they found one, replied in kind.

After each incident, Livingstone would "stalk" into the school, as Bennett put it, and complain to the principal. He calmed her down with polite attention and promised to remind his charges to exercise "courtesy and consideration," then ordered the children to leave the recluse alone.

Young Estelline burned with the unfairness, complaining to her father that Livingstone was always the one who cast the first stone.

Judge Granville Bennett calmly pointed out that the children had no business on her property and didn't even need to walk down that particular street.

Madam Henrico also sued the local Catholic Church for encroaching on her precious land's boundaries, even accusing Father Peter Rosen of assaulting her. But, in the end, according to historian Jerry Bryant, she deeded her plot to the church in 1889 and remained living there until her death in 1910.

INEZ SEXTON
Not for Sale

At the end of December 1879, singer Inez Sexton arrived in Deadwood with a variety troupe, ready to perform at Al Swearingen's Gem Theater. One of the papers soon reported that she was the "Queen of Operatic and Ballad Song" and that "no one can sing higher, lower, softer or sweeter."

When Swearingen informed Sexton that he also expected her to socialize (and more) with his customers, the singer let him know in no uncertain terms that that would not be happening: "Although my voice is for sale, nothing else is!"

Her virtuous stand endeared her to the town's proper ladies, and when Sexton suffered a serious illness they held a benefit for her (Swearingen himself was listed as one of the performers), and a Mrs. Burnham in nearby Elizabethtown opened her home to the ailing singer.

Sexton performed a few more times in Deadwood until mid-1880, when she was well enough to leave town. During that time, she received marriage proposals from John Mellor, "the Bald Mountain poet," and Woman's Dress, an Oglala Sioux who offered six ponies as a bride price.

MADAM BULLDOG
How Many Were There?

If you were traveling or driving freight between Deadwood and Custer City, you were welcome to stop for a little refreshment at the Bulldog Ranch near Rochford, southeast of Deadwood, the home of Sarah Ann and John Jacob Erb. This was not a stagecoach relay station, but after the couple moved there in September 1878, they ran a small saloon and offered hearty plates of Sarah's cooking to those who stopped. Historian Jerry L. Bryant tells much of their story in a lively *Deadwood Magazine* article.

Living right by the road had its drawbacks. Sarah didn't want passersby deciding to enjoy a stolen chicken dinner and deprive the ranch of eggs her hens had laid. So she tied two bulldogs to the henhouse—end of problem, beginning of ranch name.

Along with food and drink, travelers may have been treated to some noisy entertainment, because the Erbs had the type of marriage that would only politely be called "rocky." John was jealous and possessive, and Sarah was pretty rough around the edges. She fought back and protected herself, supposedly always carrying at least one pistol in her pockets. She also had a powerful temper and was well known on the streets of Deadwood for displaying it.

After the couple had lived at Bulldog Ranch for eleven months, their disagreements came to a head. Sarah was visiting in Deadwood, inquiring about separation or divorce and raising funds for moving there, when John apparently had had enough. He sold the ranch, then cleaned out the furniture, herded up the livestock, and delivered them for safekeeping at Ten Mile Ranch, a stage relay station southwest of Lead.

Just before that, John, who suspected his spouse of wrongdoing, had followed her around Deadwood and discovered her in the act of pawning at least one of his pistols. He saw her enter the pawnshop and opened the door to follow. Sarah was receiving the pawnbroker's assessment of the gun's value. She immediately aimed it at John, who made a quick escape, taking no chances that the pistol was loaded and she would use it. Instead, he went back to the ranch and took his revenge.

About two weeks later, the Erbs met in a judge's chambers to change their legal status and divide joint property. Later events seem to indicate that Sarah believed they were divorced, but John thought it was only a legal separation.

Sarah moved east of Rapid City on the road to Pierre, where she founded the New Bulldog Ranch and hired four hands. One of them, twenty-year-old George Hammond, was eleven years younger than Sarah and locally notorious for trying to con Deadwood businessmen by offering brass filings as genuine gold dust. Apparently Sarah and George became a couple.

The following year, 1880, John Erb went to the law in Deadwood and accused Sarah of bigamy, naming Hammond. Gale Hill, the man gravely wounded when the Monitor treasure coach was robbed at Canyon Springs, was the deputy sheriff sent to the New Bulldog to serve the papers. Sarah greeted Hill with a revolver, while George held a shotgun on the lawman. Hill went back to Deadwood alone.

Soon, W. S. Fanshawe, who ran the Fort Meade post store, sued Sarah for $700 she owed on her account. He was afraid she would leave the country to evade John's bigamy charge. Two soldiers deputized to collect Sarah were instead politely paid the $700—no guns in sight.

Sarah's bigamy trial in January 1881 ended in her acquittal, but a year later she was arrested for buying buffalo coats stolen from soldiers. Two days later, she was again charged with buying stolen property offered by a soldier, and arraigned for trial. She had recently sold the New Bulldog and moved back to Deadwood, opening a saloon named—what else?—the Bulldog. Not surprisingly, in March she was charged with assault and battery, likely on a patron. After this, Sarah Erb gave up on Deadwood and moved to Miles City, Montana Territory, where she began working as a poker dealer.

Trying to follow Sarah after she left the Hills (and Bryant's biography ends) leads to a Madam Bulldog who appeared at Sunnydale, north of the railroad town of Livingston, Montana, in 1885. (Sunnydale was later renamed Clyde Park in honor of its setting and a local ranch that bred Clydesdale horses.) This Madam Bulldog ran a stage station, and in 1887, when a post office opened within, its postmistress was one Sarah Robinson.

South of Sunnydale sat the town of Livingston, founded by the Northern Pacific Railway in 1882 as both a division point and the line's gateway to Yellowstone National Park. With many railroaders having to stay overnight in town, Livingston soon boasted an array of boardinghouses, saloons, brothels, and dance halls to serve the railroaders and also cowboys from surrounding ranches.

A Madam Bulldog opened a saloon there called the Bucket of Blood—a not uncommon Wild West bar name—and possibly attached a dance hall and brothel to it. She gave her name as "Kitty O'Leary," and people assumed that her nickname of Madam Bulldog fitted her heavy weight and short stature. Little else is known about this Madam Bulldog, but one wonders whether she was Sarah Erb, still trying to hide from her vindictive ex-husband.

MRS. BRENNAN
You Can't Talk to My Son That Way
In 1880, Deadwood's four-year-old school system consisted of a single two-story building where the sixty or so pupils were taught by the principal, Dolph Edwards, and Miss Eva Deffenbacher.

One day, a boy named Brennan was disagreeing with another student and drew a knife to bolster his argument. Mr. Edwards and Miss Deffenbacher heartily objected.

Mrs. Brennan, the boy's mother, apparently did not mind his behavior. To make her protest against the faculty, mom soon showed up at the building armed with both pistol and whip—a clear case of like mother, like son. It took a while for Mr. Edwards to convince her not to use either weapon, but all ended well for staff and pupils.

MRS. HAYES
Mother of the Badlands
In the 1880s, Estelline Bennett recounts, the widowed Mrs. Hayes lived in a small ramshackle building next door to Pete's Place, a Deadwood badlands district saloon. On summer days she sat out front offering fruit for sale, rocking and nodding off in her chair. She spread out her wares in mid-afternoon and stayed at her post until Main Street emptied in the early morning hours.

Along with fresh fruit, Mrs. Hayes offered the district's wild women a shoulder to cry on and an ear to hear their tales of woe. Sometimes the working girls parked their children with the widow while they went off on benders with their beaux of the moment. The children were fed and cared for during the interim. Bennett termed the fruitseller the "mother of the badlands."

Mrs. Hayes once had worked as a maid in the home of Bennett relatives, back in Kansas, who even hosted her wedding in their home.

Widowhood came when a man threw a heavy glass stein at her husband in a bar, killing him instantly. The thrower was acquitted because the men had been arguing over a poker game, and a beer stein could not be considered a deadly weapon. That man, a brewer, had then supported Mrs. Hayes until his own death.

In the 1870s, historian Jerry Bryant notes, Mrs. Hayes ran a fruit stand and confectionary in Lead, receiving goods from Bismarck, which supported her and an assistant. She even contributed money for Deadwood's Fourth of July celebration.

For curious young Estelline, daughter of a judge, Mrs. Hayes was a source of some information on the mysterious doings of the forbidden badlands district—sanitized, no doubt. The widow complained about her own reputation, knowing that people said she dozed in her rocking chair because she was drunk. She didn't drink, she swore to Estelline—and besides, if she did, she still could attend to business better than some of Deadwood's male shopkeepers.

The girl worried about Mrs. Hayes's shabby clothing and finally appealed to her mother for a used garment to give her friend. After all, Mrs. Hayes was connected to their family, she argued. An old green sateen day dress was mended and cleaned, and Estelline delightedly delivered it.

Soon afterward, Mrs. Bennett happened to be at her window that looked down the steep side of the gulch onto the lower end of Main Street. She saw her green dress come out of the back of Pete's Place, its wearer carrying a bucket of beer to the back door of her own dilapidated house next door.

"I never thought I would come to this," said Mrs. Bennett. "Coming out of the back of the saloon carrying 'a bucket of something.'"

Estelline happily enlightened her, showing off her knowledge of contemporary slang: "By to-night it will be all over town that Mrs. Bennett has taken to rushing the can to Pete's Place."

Her mother pretended not even to hear.

SUE NEILL
"I Did Not Intend To Come in Here"
Illustrating how respected and firm was the line between good women

and wild women, Estelline Bennett tells the story of one of the former making a minor mistake that drew a profound reaction.

Sue Neill was the "tall, witty, red-haired spinster who remained county superintendent of schools no matter what party was in power." One evening in the 1880s, Neill was heading down Main Street to the *Black Hills Pioneer* office to place a notice about county teacher examinations, and she must have been thinking of something else entirely. Bennett recounts:

> She went through an open door and looked around for desks, green-shaded lamps, and industrious scribblers. Instead, she found herself in the midst of faro layouts, poker tables, and roulette wheels. She gave one startled sweeping glance around and then smiled pleasantly at the astonished but friendly looking white-aproned man who gazed at her in amazement, the napkin in his hand poised in startled surprise above the mahogany bar he had been polishing. Half a dozen little drinks were held in suspense halfway between the bar and half a dozen drooping mustaches.
>
> "I assure you, gentlemen," Miss Neill said easily, "I did not intend to come in here. It was a mistake."
>
> The bartender dropped his napkin and bowed low. "I'm sure of that, Madam," he said. "The Pioneer *office is next door.*"
>
> They bowed formally to each other again and everybody else bowed, and the lady withdrew.

MAGGIE LAUGHLIN
Not Now, Calamity, Not Now!

Maggie Laughlin had been a dance hall girl in Deadwood during the Black Hills gold rush, where she knew and worked with Calamity Jane; it is not known whether she also was a prostitute. Calamity was making her slow, wandering return from New York in 1901—after a failed vaudeville tour and wasting her travel money on drink—and stopped in Pierre, South Dakota. She knew that Laughlin had gotten married and lived there now so, a quarter century after they last had visited, Calamity Jane decided to call on her old friend and have a reunion. She first, of course, got "drunker than a hoot owl," according to Charles Fales, as quoted by historian James McLaird.

But the now-respectable Laughlin happened to be entertaining the ladies of her church that afternoon. She had to scurry to get the loud and crude visitor away from her home as quickly as possible, and one wonders how she explained the intrusion, or that she even knew such a notorious wild woman.

POKER ALICE TUBBS
Scandalous but Forgiven

Poker Alice Tubbs carved out a decent living for herself as a professional gambler, apparently never having to stoop to dancing or prostitution. But, of course, in the Victorian era she was nowhere near respectable, because of her line of work.

Poker Alice didn't arrive in the Black Hills until after its placer gold heyday, showing up around 1890.

The beautiful, intelligent, and well-educated Alice Ivers was born in the early 1850s. She claimed to be English-born and in her teens when the family emigrated to the United States, first settling in Virginia and then moving permanently to Colorado. But research by Mildred Fields, her biographer, indicates that Alice was born in Virginia of Irish immigrants who had lived in England at one time; at the time, Irish immigrants were considered far less desirable than English ones.

Alice somehow found her way to Colorado, where she met and married mining engineer Frank Duffield when she was in her early twenties.

It was quite the liberated marriage for its day. Frank liked to play poker, and pretty soon Alice was going along to the gambling parlors and playing against her husband and other men. She became quite skilled, adept at figuring the odds, counting cards, and reading the other players—all while keeping the requisite "poker face."

After Frank was killed in a mine accident, the young widow turned professional poker player to support herself. She soon learned to protect herself by carrying, displaying, and being willing to use a small handgun.

Alas, no photograph is known to exist of Poker Alice Tubbs in her younger, stylish days. But the quality of her thick, warm sweater seems to indicate she was well off in her later years, as one who earned a quarter of a million dollars should have been.

At the tables, Alice also discovered the joys of cigar smoking, and her stogies became a trademark. Either then or later, she also developed a fondness for drinking.

The lady gambler enjoyed fine clothing and maintained a stylish wardrobe. She never appeared in anything but finely fitted dresses, and well into her fifties she was still considered quite the handsome woman.

Poker Alice worked mainly in Colorado and New Mexico before moving to Deadwood in her forties.

She met Warren G. Tubbs, her second husband, at Deadwood's tables. He was a Sturgis house painter and sometime poker dealer. Even after their wedding, they played against each other, with Alice's luck and skill much higher than her spouse's. She once claimed that she never cheated (because she didn't need to) and that her lifetime winnings were a quarter of a million dollars.

When their seven children began to come along, the pair left the poker tables and homesteaded near Sturgis. They lived there for what proved to be the last years of Warren Tubbs's life, and Poker Alice nursed her husband as he faded away from tuberculosis. After his death in 1910, Alice buried her second husband in Sturgis and went back to work to support the homestead. She hired George Huckert to manage it in her absence. They soon married, but Alice was widowed for the third and final time in 1913. She continued to call herself Tubbs for the rest of her life.

Black Hills saloons and gambling parlors had become a lot more scarce since Alice's retirement from the poker tables. Starting a new career as she entered her sixties, Poker Alice opened a brothel near Fort Meade, the cavalry post that had opened in 1878 east of Sturgis. She bought an existing home, then used bank loans to add rooms and to travel to Kansas City, where she recruited six prostitutes. She paid off the bank within two years.

Poker Alice didn't intend to run a low-class, rowdy place. When some soldiers started running amok in 1913, she pulled out a rifle, intending to shoot over their heads and shock them into quietness. But she hit two men, and one died, resulting in a murder trial. She was acquitted after testimony about the dead man's wild actions.

Tubbs carried on the business, paying fines as necessary, serving occasional jail time as a madam, and ignoring Prohibition during the 1920s, but eventually she would receive a gubernatorial pardon at the age of seventy-five years. She also appeared, by invitation, in Deadwood's Days of '76 parade, after it began in the 1920s. Poker Alice Tubbs died in 1930, by then celebrated as a colorful original pioneer, with all her sins forgiven. →

CHAPTER EIGHT

TALL-TALE TELLERS

WILLIAM F. "BUFFALO BILL" CODY
Shooting, Fighting Wild West Shows

Buffalo Bill Cody seems to have been born to become a successful showman, always doing his work with a dramatic flair—and happy to act it out in public with additional flourishes and curlicues. According to Agnes Wright Spring, early freighters who worked around Cody nicknamed him "See Me Bill" for the way he enjoyed showing off.

The "Buffalo" moniker came when he was a meat hunter for railroad crews, riding the Plains and killing bison to feed them. Later, Buffalo Bill Cody worked as a scout for the U.S. Army during its summer campaigns against the Indians. In the winters, beginning in 1872, he went east to appear in stage melodramas that exaggerated his own career and helped fix the Wild West image in the nation's imagina-

William F. Cody first earned his status as an exceptional frontiersman by doing the real—and dangerous—work, then made fame but not fortune as a showman for more than three decades. DENVER PUBLIC LIBRARY, NS-243.

tion. For thirty-two seasons, beginning in 1883, his touring Wild West show took the romanticized frontier to cities and towns across North America and northern Europe. For most of those years he ran it alone, calling it Buffalo Bill's Wild West and Congress of Rough Riders of the World.

Cody's closest personal connection with the Black Hills came south of them, in 1876, at Hat Creek, which the Black Hills Trail crossed en route to Deadwood. An Indian fight resulted in an act for his show, "The First Scalp for Custer." Cody had come by train to Cheyenne to scout for Colonel Wesley Merritt's 5th Cavalry, which was to reinforce General George Crook's command in what is now called the Great Sioux War. Troops in columns arriving from three directions—under General Alfred Terry, Colonel George Custer, and Crook—were to push "non-treaty" Sioux and Northern Cheyenne people out of their Montana-Wyoming Powder River hunting lands and back onto the Sioux reservation in South Dakota and Nebraska.

Merritt's 5th Cavalry had belatedly left southern Wyoming to join Crook when Cody caught up with them. On June 18, in Montana Territory, General Crook lost to the Sioux and Cheyenne on Rosebud Creek. Exactly one week later, Custer led five of the 7th Cavalry's twelve companies to oblivion on the Little Bighorn River in Montana (while Indians pinned down the other seven companies, preventing them from riding to Custer's aid), at the hands of many of the same Sioux and Cheyenne warriors. Still in Wyoming, Merritt—and Cody—didn't learn of Custer's fate until July 6, through a field dispatch.

Eight days later, Merritt heard that a large group of Northern Cheyenne were leaving the Red Cloud Agency in Nebraska. He decided to pause and head them off rather than continue north toward Crook. With Cody as scout, Merritt's troops reached Hat Creek in two days and awaited the Cheyennes.

Just as the Cheyennes came into view, so did army couriers trying to reach Merritt. Seven Cheyenne warriors peeled off after the approaching couriers. Cody, another scout, and six soldiers went after the Cheyennes. When they reached them, Cody shot one warrior through the leg and killed his horse; the warrior's shot at Cody missed. When Cody's horse stumbled on a prairie dog hole, he jumped off, knelt, and killed the warrior. Then he scalped him.

Cody always called his victim Yellow Hand, but the Northern Cheyenne people, and contemporary army reports, name him Yellow Hair. Cody dramatically labeled his deed taking "the first scalp for Custer" and reenacted it in his later Wild West show.

Although Cody knew and wrote about some of Deadwood's prominent residents, including Wild Bill Hickok and Calamity Jane, he seems never to have visited that Black Hills mining camp. But including the popular act "The Rescue of the Deadwood Stage" in his performances probably led many audiences to think he was very familiar with the place.

CAPTAIN JACK CRAWFORD
The Poet Scout

When he was nearly seventy years old and dying on Long Island, New York, Captain Jack Crawford summarized his life for an interviewer: "I was simply a boy soldier, rustic poet, and a bad actor." That statement, while not untrue, left out a great deal.

His full name, John Wallace Crawford, honored his mother's proud descent from William Wallace, the fourteenth-century Scottish knight who rebelled against the English crown. Young Jack was seven in 1854 when his family emigrated from Ireland to the coal country of western Pennsylvania. There his father worked in the mines as much as he could—and stayed drunk.

Jack and his brothers took up the slack by working in coal mines instead of going to school. They likely were human beasts of burden, crawling through narrow tunnels on their hands and knees while wearing special harnesses that pulled carts heaped with coal—a mining job open to children and women.

At age fourteen, Jack saw the Civil War as an escape from underground and joined the Union army. He served throughout the war, until being severely wounded twice as the war's end neared. While he recovered in a Sisters of Charity hospital, a nun taught the young man how to read and write. He would combine the new skills with the tradition of Irish storytelling to make his living from then on.

Returning to Pennsylvania, he began working as a newspaper reporter and supported his mother until her death a few years later. He vowed to her never to drink alcohol and not only kept the promise but also preached the teetotaling life to all and sundry he met over the years.

In 1869 he married Maria Stokes, and they began a family that would include three children. Frontier adventures called, and Crawford moved to Nebraska seven years later. He found work as an *Omaha Bee* correspondent and then was sent to the Black Hills in 1875 by the *Sidney Telegraph* (Nebraska). His reports on the army's attempt to evict prospectors that year were published by many eastern newspapers.

Crawford fell in love with the Hills and in 1876 seriously involved himself in Deadwood. He got onto the city council and became captain of the town's Indian-fighting Black Hills Rangers when it organized. While still filing newspaper stories, he also served as an army scout and messenger, working with Buffalo Bill Cody in the service of General Wesley Merritt. The latter's troops joined George Crook's forces after the Battle of the Little Bighorn of June 1876. After this service, Crawford became known as "The Poet Scout of the Black Hills."

In his autobiography, Cody credited Crawford with delivering a bottle of whiskey from an officer in Cheyenne, a gift to Cody in the field. He wrote, "Jack is the only man I have ever known that could have brought that bottle of whiskey through without accident befalling it, for he is one of the very few teetotal scouts I ever met."

After Cody left the troops to return east in the fall, he hired Crawford to join his acting troupe. (Buffalo Bill's Wild West and Congress of Rough Riders of the World was still six years in the future.) Jack played himself, but that was about the end of art imitating life. As always, Cody had a playwright take one event and turn it into a grand stage spectacle.

By now, Crawford was writing and publishing poetry. If he didn't invent the genre of cowboy poetry, he was one of its first practitioners, but he also wrote a sentimental verse that was widely published at the time. This touching "Mother's Prayers" was one of Crawford's better-finished works and became one of his most popular. Recalling how his mother prayed for his childhood safety and righteousness, the poet tells how, later,

And when danger hovered o'er me
And when life was full of cares,
Then a sweet form passed before me
And I thought of Mother's prayers.

Crawford claimed that Wild Bill Hickok told him the poem struck "a tender spot" with him.

He also joined many other American poets in lamenting George Custer's death in 1876, using his frontier persona:

Did I hear the news from Custer?
Well, I reckon I did, old pard.
It came like a streak o' lightning,
And you bet, it hit me hard.
I ain't no hand to blubber,
And the briny ain't run for years,
But chalk me down for a lubber
If I didn't shed regular tears.

Crawford toured with Cody until July 1877, when he accidentally shot himself in the groin during an on-stage battle scene. He rejoined Cody briefly in 1879, in the cast of a play touring the Pacific Coast and Northwest. But the two had a major shouting match in San Francisco after a benefit performance on Crawford's behalf didn't pull in as much money as Crawford had hoped. Cody's hearty drinking also probably caused friction between the two.

Writing to an old friend in 1879, Cody included Crawford in a list of frontiersmen who had worked with him on stage who "just as soon as they see their names in print a few times they git the big head and want to start a company of their own" and fail because they have no idea how to run such a business.

Crawford never returned to live in the Black Hills after working with Cody. He moved his family to New Mexico Territory in 1879. He combined running Fort Craig's trading post, near Socorro, with prospecting, ranching, and a little show biz. There was good money to be made on the "platform lecture" circuit, where speakers might recite poems, comment on the current scene, reminisce, or offer skill demonstrations. Leaving his wife with a shotgun to defend herself and the children, Crawford would travel the circuit from time to time and was popular with eastern audiences. Although Maria pronounced his costume "silly," Crawford appeared in heavily beaded and fur-trimmed buckskins, with a wide-brimmed sombrero over his long hair. He recited poems and possibly some of the three hundred short stories he would publish and gave shooting demonstrations that supposedly re-created actual fights.

In the 1890s, Crawford seriously hit the road as a performer, one of the most popular lecturers around. Sometime during these years, Maria moved out, and they never lived together again.

When he appeared in Rapid City in 1893, he wrote a special poem to the city, calling it the "Foothills Queen." Seeing how the town was evolving into a modern city made him nostalgic, and he offered residents this warning:

> Remember Rome was not erected in a day
> You may be Rapid, yet I thought it strange
> That some were roaring for a rabid change…
> Be Rapid always—but be not too fast.

The thought of a big gold strike apparently hadn't left the Poet Scout's mind, because he joined the Klondike gold rush in 1898, giving up his New Mexico ranch. Captain Jack returned, broke, after two fruitless years in the Klondike, and continued to make a living with voice and pen. In the early 1910s, he even wrote for and appeared in some silent films.

When the Poet Scout died of kidney disease in New York in 1917, he ranked among the many who had outlived the frontier they loved. John H. "Ranger" Pierce, whom he knew from the Black Hills, eulogized him in sad acknowledgment of the fact:

> Jack Crawford, poet-scout.
> So you are mustered out.
> Goodbye, old Captain Jack,
> I loved you, but I would not bring you back.

DIME NOVELS
Yellow-Back Seducers of Youth

From the dime novel *Deadwood Dick's Doom; or, Calamity Jane's Last Adventure*, by Edward L. Wheeler:

Calamity had changed but little since the time when this pen last introduced her: she was the same graceful, pretty girl-in-breeches that she had always been, but if there was any change it was in the sterner expression of her sad eyes.

A murmur of "Calamity Jane," ran through the bar-room as she entered, proving that she was recognized by more than one.

"Yes Calamity Jane!" she retorted. "I see I am not unknown even in this strange place. Better perhaps, is it so, for you'll have a clearer idea of whom you have to deal with. I want to know where Deadwood Dick is what I want. I allow ye'll say he ain't here, but I won't swallow that. He told me he'd be here, over a week ago, an' he allus keeps his dates."

"An' so you are wantin' him, eh?" Piute Dave grunted, from his perch on one end of the bar. "S'pose likely you're a pard o' his'n eh?"

"I allow I've been his truest pard for many a year," Calamity replied, "but that's not what I was asking. Where is Deadwood Dick?"

"Well, gal, ef my memory serves me right, I allow the last I see'd o' him he was a sinkin' in a bed of quicksand, where I throwed him. We had a tassel, an' ther best man was ter chuck t'other 'un in the quicksand, an' ther honor fell onto me. He weakened and I give him a boost, an' I presume ef he's kept right on sinkin' ever since he's arriv' down ter ther maiden kentry o' the washee washee [homeland of the Chinese], by this time."

Calamity's heart sunk within her at this declaration but outwardly she was very calm.

She had met Deadwood Dick in the lower mining

districts, a few weeks before, and he had said, as he took her hand in his, in parting:

"I'm going up to Death Notch, Janie, on my last adventuresome trail, and after that I'm going to settle down for good, in some lonely spot and see if the remainder of my life cannot be passed in more peace and quiet than the past has been. Come to me, at Death Notch, Calamity and the hand you have so long sought shall be yours. We will go hence down the avenue of life, hand in hand together as man and wife."

The real Calamity Jane's personality, life, and loves were nothing like that, but the dime novel heroine Calamity Jane was quite another, and purely fictional, story.

Spies, detectives, Secret Service agents, sailors and pirates on the high seas, grizzled mountain men, cowboys and a few cowgirls, marshals, gunfighters, anachronistically independent noblewomen and their gallant knights—they all appeared in dime novels, America's first mass market paperbacks that flourished from 1860 into the 1890s. The fiction was sensational without being explicit, filled with plenty of action scenes, and each exciting small book sold for either a dime or a nickel. Volumes in ongoing series, like the Deadwood Dick books, found ways, time and again, to "discover" that the hero actually was alive after being killed off in the previous volume.

Authors included women as well as men, many writing under pen names or without a byline at all. *Little Women* author Louisa May Alcott, determined to make her living by her pen, wrote several pseudonymous and anonymous dime novels over the years.

More than one young man who made his way to the Black Hills had been inspired by the violent derring-do of dime novels and expected life there to be somewhat like what he'd read. Little did he know that some of the books' authors had never experienced the Wild West.

Calamity Jane became more famous for being a dime novel heroine than for her own shabby deeds, beginning in 1877 when a character with that generic name appeared in the very first Deadwood Dick series entry. Jane both hated the phony claptrap written about her and was willing to use it to make her living, or at least to cadge some free drinks. In the novels, Calamity Jane was athletic, honorable, and sensitive—a fighter for justice. She had a temper, as did Deadwood Dick, guaranteeing that they broke up and reconciled in story after story—even after their fictional characters had wed and produced a son, Deadwood Dick, Jr.

Meanwhile, young people, especially the urban working class, loved the thrillers and kept their major publisher, Beadle and Adams, and other companies busy cranking them out. The books were easy to find, sold from newsstands instead of bookstores. Educated adults generally scorned such writing for the masses, making it even more delicious for the youthful smart set.

Beadle and Adams invented the series name "Dime Novels" and printed so many of their titles between yellow covers that "yellow-backed book" became another synonym for the action literature; in Britain, where the penny had greater monetary value, such books were known as "penny dreadfuls." Beadle and Adams added a Half-Dime Novel series to its catalog, and among these were the Deadwood Dick titles.

The dime novel largely began to fail when a great economic depression affected the country in the mid-1890s. At the same time, printing technology allowed magazines to add grainy photographs, making these publications much more interesting. But the dime novels had been around at the right time to fictionalize the brief days of cowboys on trail drives, stagecoach and train robberies, and gunfights in the streets of Deadwood. Their authors created characters, situations, and images that later filmmakers (the first silent film with a plot, *The Great Train Robbery*, was set in the West) and television producers would repeat and carve into American pop culture.

DEADWOOD DICK
Who Was He Really?
In 1877, the character Deadwood Dick came straight out of the imagination of Edward L. Wheeler, a successful dime novelist, but several living, breathing men over the years have claimed the fictional persona for their own glory, money, or just the fun of it.

Probably more than one man claimed the nickname while still living in Deadwood. Jeannine P. Guern states that one Cheyenne and Black Hills Stage Line driver, "Little Dick" Cole, tried to get folks to call him "Deadwood Dick" because he thought it would help stave off bandits. It certainly was more glamorous than the stocky Cornishman's own sobriquet, but the other drivers couldn't be bothered with calling Cole by the new name. No problem, though, because Cole was an excellent hand with a gun, and his coach was never robbed of gold.

Nat Love's autobiography, as we see below, claims that Deadwood residents spontaneously bestowed the moniker on him.

Historian Jerry Bryant credits Richard Bullock with being the original incarnation of Deadwood Dick—although he hadn't been known by the name when he lived in Deadwood. He was a great marksman and was well known around Deadwood and Lead for defending gold shipments from highway robbers. Bullock lived in Deadwood from 1878 until he moved on to California in 1896, claiming the nickname later in life to capitalize on the fictional hero's fame. Bullock lived to the ripe age of seventy-five, dying in Glendale, California, in 1920.

Richard Clark was the longest-lived Deadwood-Dick-in-the-flesh, his fame accepted and spread by newspaper reporters who hadn't checked more deeply than Clark's own press releases. An English immigrant, he had been in Deadwood during its heyday (and was seen in Colorado Charlie Utter's company), but it wasn't until the late 1890s that local businessmen began presenting him as the "true Deadwood Dick."

Clark had carried express mail on the Fort Pierre route, ridden as a shotgun messenger on the same route's stagecoaches, and held a job in a Lead livery stable. He spent most of his career working for one of the Hills' narrow-gauge railroads.

Being a good Black Hills resident, he also mined on the side. In 1898, he seriously injured himself in a blasting explosion, breaking both arms and some ribs, among other injuries. While he was in the Homestake Hospital at Lead, eastern newspapers picked up the story and referred to Clark as the famous dime novel hero.

After that, Clark spent years happily wearing his hair long, dressing in buckskins, and serving as ambassador for the local businesses. He received celebrity guests and other tourists and traveled the country promoting Deadwood Gulch. He even went to Washington, D.C., in 1928 to thank President Calvin Coolidge for visiting the Hills the previous year and to invite him to return.

Coolidge, having wanted a peaceful, healthful vacation away from the heat and humidity of Foggy Bottom, had set up his summer White House from June into August at Rapid City. He was there to relax and catch trout, not to make public appearances, and apparently he didn't visit Deadwood— although Gutzon Borglum did talk the reluctant president into "dedicating" Mount Rushmore for the carvings Borglum was undertaking.

"Deadwood Dick" Clark died in 1930, his funeral a great public tribute with cavalry buglers playing "Taps," a gun salute, and an aeroplane passing overhead to drop roses on his Sunrise Mountain grave.

NAT LOVE
Red River Dick, Deadwood Dick & George

Nat Love claimed, in his 1907 autobiography, that he was one of the cowboys riding attendance on 3,000 Arizona longhorns driven to Deadwood in 1876, which arrived in town on July 3. The next day he said he relaxed at a local rodeo-style competition, where he made quite a showing and, according to that romanticized book, received the nickname "Deadwood Dick." Twenty-two years old that year, he had already been cowboying for a third of his life.

Sadly, historian Jerry Bryant has been unable to find any contemporary mention of Love's claim. However, the story has become so widespread that it must be considered—even though it may have been only a wistful creation on Love's part. Love's life, however, as a reflection on his times, remains worth telling as he presented it.

Love noted that six other African Americans competed in that Fourth of July roping contest, but not whether he was the only black cowboy traveling in his own outfit. He'd gone to the Kansas frontier when nearly fifteen years old, in 1869, and quickly was hired on—then had to learn horsemanship, roping, and shooting. Love mastered those skills quickly and thoroughly.

He'd been born on the Robert Love tobacco plantation near Nashville, Tennessee, sometime in June 1854, the youngest of three children. He

Even though he wasn't the Deadwood Dick of fiction, or "the first black cowboy," as some have called him, Nat Love was the authentic article, a working cowhand who endured the hardships and enjoyed the freedoms of the cowboy life. SOUTH DAKOTA HISTORICAL SOCIETY, STATE ARCHIVES.

wrote, "The exact date of my birth I never knew, because in those days no count was kept of such trivial matters as the birth of a slave baby." His parents were both slaves holding high-level jobs, his father "a sort of foreman of the slaves" and his mother the plantation home's head cook. Surreptitiously in their cabin, Nat's father taught sister Sally, brother Jordan, and young Nat what little he knew of reading and writing.

During the Civil War, Robert Love took Nat's father with him as he served in the Confederate army, "building forts," but the father returned home safely after Union forces under General Ulysses Grant had taken the Nashville area. Robert Love had not informed his slaves of the Emancipation Proclamation in 1863, or even that the Civil War ended two years later, but he taught them to fear Yankee soldiers. To their amazement, Jordan and Nat learned that the worst the invading forces would do to them was take their food—still a great hardship for the slaves, whose diet at best consisted of mostly bran and pork-skin cracklings. Nat's mother turned the former into "ash cakes" by making dough with milk or water and a little salt, wrapping the cakes in cabbage leaves, and baking them in the bottom of the fireplace.

Even after news of freedom finally reached the Love plantation, life there went on the same. Now the former slaves were sharecroppers, renting their land and endlessly in debt to Robert Love. In 1869, young Nat decided to head west and see what work he could find, hoping for better wages than the $1.50 per month he then was earning.

In Dodge City, Kansas, Nat Love hired on with the Duval outfit from Texas, which he said included several "colored cow boys," and was taught the necessary skills by "Bronko Jim," another African American. Love was tested by being given a wild horse to ride; when he hung on and rode the steed to a standstill, he became a cowboy trainee with the pay of $30 a month. Bronko Jim called the teenager "Red River Dick," a nickname Love used for years.

By the time he competed in Deadwood, Love was an experienced cowboy, and that Fourth of July he demonstrated it. For the roping competition, twelve entrants (half of them black) lined up, each assigned a wild mustang that he had to rope, throw, tie, bridle, saddle, and then ride. The one who did all that quickest would claim a $200 purse put up by businessmen and miners. Love spent nine minutes achieving the goal; the second-place finisher needed twelve and a half minutes. (Writing his autobiography in 1907, Love said that his record still stood.) Awarding him the purse, the crowd declared that henceforth Red River Dick would be known as Deadwood Dick. Love used his prize to treat his compadres and wrote that, for several days, "the purse…went toward keeping things moving, and they did move as only a large crowd of cattle men can move things."

That afternoon's shooting competition was an impromptu affair set up after some cowboys began debating who was best with a rifle and who with a revolver. For no prize except bragging rights, competitors shot both types of gun fourteen times at a target—250 yards away for rifles and 100 yards for six-shooters. Love placed all his rifle shots in the bull's-eye, but only ten of his revolver shots. Still, he was the winner; Stormy Jim, the local champion, came in second with eight rifle and five revolver bull's-eyes.

Nat Love continued cowboying in the Southwest, with trips into Mexico and north to U.S. cattle towns, until 1890. The business had changed by then, and he left it regretfully; in his autobiography, he uses the phrase "wild and free" again and again to describe the cowboy life. He had married in 1889, and the following year he went to work as a Pullman porter on the Denver and Rio Grande Railroad, assigned to the run between Denver and Salida, Colorado. He and his wife, Alice, lived in the former city and eventually added a daughter to their family. Besides buying his own uniform for $22, Love had to get a letter from a banker verifying his account before he could become a Pullman man.

Now his work nickname became "George," for George Pullman, who had invented the sleeping car in 1867. In the Pullman Company's early years, all its sleeping car workers were African Americans, and riders wanting to summon any of them traditionally called for "George."

Love didn't last long during his first term as a porter, angered when he got no tips (and grumpy or swearing comments) after he mixed up all the shoes left out overnight for him to polish. He resigned and soon bought a horse and wagon from which he sold fruit, vegetables, honey, and chickens around Denver. He was satisfied with this income, but the work was boring. At least, Love decided, being a Pullman porter included interesting travel and potential excitement, so he rejoined the company.

This was the beginning of a long and relatively lucrative career, for now Nat Love applied himself to giving good service—"service not servitude," according to a motto of Pullman porters. He traveled throughout the United States, with most long-distance passengers adding a $10 tip to his monthly salary of $40. When he served as head porter on a specially commissioned car, he might receive a tip, or "purse," as he called it, of $100 to $150 from the sponsoring group.

Nat Love, retired from Pullman service, died at the age of sixty-seven in Los Angeles.

EDWARD L. WHEELER
Creator of Deadwood Dick

Despite fancy letterhead that proclaimed him a "sensational novelist" (meaning author of thrillers) who was writing from his "studio" in Philadelphia, Edward L. Wheeler shared the working-class background of many of his readers. He was born in New York in 1854 or 1855 and grew up helping in his family's boardinghouse in the oil boomtown of Titusville, Pennsylvania. The family later moved to Philadelphia, where they took in boarders attending the U.S. centennial celebration in 1876.

By the mid-1870s, the teenage Wheeler had begun a writing career for the "story papers," periodicals that published adventure fiction. That brought him a contract, in 1877, to produce the first work in Beadle and Adams's new Half-Dime Library imprint: *Deadwood Dick, the Prince of the Road; or, the Black Rider of the Black Hills*. The series was a success, and Wheeler went on to write thirty-three Deadwood Dick novels, earning a comfortable living for himself and his wife, Alice. The couple lived in Philadelphia suburbs, with some occasional stays back in Titusville.

The author never traveled to the Black Hills, and he blithely rearranged the geography of Deadwood Gulch and its surroundings to suit his fiction's needs.

Wheeler also wrote other series, under other pen names, but his personal life remains obscure. Albert Johannsen, an avid collector and bibliographer of dime novels, concluded that Wheeler died in 1885, around the age of thirty. The Deadwood Dick character died then, too, but a new series of Deadwood Dick, Jr. novels began—written by someone else but carrying Wheeler's byline.

Johannsen himself (1871–1962) is intriguing, a geologist who worked in the West for the U.S. Geological Survey before joining the faculty of the University of Chicago. He personally collected most of the more than seven thousand Beadle and Adams paperbacks, and in 1950 the University of Oklahoma Press published his book, which gives the company's history, lists all its titles, and sorts out the maze of pen names under which stories were published.

Here is the first glimpse of Deadwood Dick, as written by Wheeler:

> He was a youth of an age somewhere between sixteen and twenty, trim and compactly built, with a preponderance of muscular development and animal spirits; broad and deep of chest, with square, iron-cast shoulders; limbs small yet like bars of steel, and with a grace of position in the saddle rarely equaled; he made a fine picture for an artist's brush or a poet's pen.
>
> Only one thing marred the captivating beauty of the picture.
>
> His form was clothed in a tight-fitting habit of buck-skin, which was colored a jetty black, and presented a striking contrast to anything one sees as a garment in the wild far West. And this was not all, either. A broad black hat was slouched down over his eyes; he wore a thick black veil over the upper portion of his face, through the eye-holes of which there gleamed a pair of orbs of piercing intensity, and his hands, large and knotted, were hidden in a pair of kid gloves of a light color.
>
> The "Black Rider" he might have been justly termed, for his thoroughbred steed was as black as coal, but we have not seen fit to call him such—his name is Deadwood Dick, and let that suffice for the present.

In this road agent disguise, Deadwood Dick commits an actual stagecoach robbery. But, never fear, the victims are an uncle and cousin who killed his parents back east, have now come to Deadwood to finish him off, and on whom the Black Rider will wreak long-overdue revenge. Calamity Jane appears in the novel a few times, coming to Dick's and others' aid, but at book's end she turns down Dick's first, of many, proposals of marriage.

EDWARD ZANE CARROLL JUDSON
Ned Buntline

Edward Judson was a born writer and an adventurer who brought actual knowledge of the sea and, to a degree, the frontier to his many dime novels. He published his first fictional sketch in a national publication at the age of seventeen, while serving in the U.S. Navy, and continued writing fiction, poetry, plays, and articles until the year before his death.

He ultimately wrote at least four hundred novels—sometimes, he claimed, working at the pace of ten thousand words of snappy dialogue and wild action a day—under a series of pen names, the best known being "Ned Buntline." He published relatively few westerns, but his self-promotion made his name one of the more famous in the genre.

Rather than become a Philadelphia lawyer like his father, Judson ran away to sea when he was thirteen. He crewed on a ship that delivered fruit from the West Indies to the New York market. After four years of service, his ship was in the East River at New York when a ferry collided with a smaller boat, dumping people into the water. Judson's heroics in saving several of them came to the attention of the navy and earned him a midshipman's commission. There he served until he was twenty-one, in 1842.

Judson claimed that he spent the following two years on the western frontier, working for the Northwest Fur Company in the area of Yellowstone National Park part of that time.

Meanwhile, he continued publishing stories, now under what became his most prominent pseudonym—Ned Buntline, named after a stabilizing rope in a sailing ship's rigging. But stability was not a large part of the volatile, red-headed Judson's own life. Sometime before 1842 he married the first of what would total six wives, a Cuban woman who died in 1846. He lost his third wife in childbirth, but numbers two, four, and five divorced the writer, with the second wife obtaining custody of their child. It seems that Judson twice remarried a bit prematurely—before his previous divorce was final.

With wife number four, Kate Myers, he produced four children during an eleven-year marriage. Judson was married to the sixth woman, Anna Fuller, for fifteen years, and they had two children. She became his widow in 1886. Historian William B. Shillingberg states that Judson and wife number two were remarried ten years after their divorce, split up again, and seem never to have divorced formally a second time.

Short and hefty, Judson was a boisterous, energetic hustler who founded several short-lived magazines early in his post-navy career. His eye for the ladies led to a duel in 1846 in which he killed Robert Porterfield, who believed he was defending his own wife's honor. An angry mob converged on Judson in a Nashville hotel, where he escaped through a third-floor window—then fell to the porch. As he lay stunned from his injuries, the mob caught him and attached the noose, but a friend cut the rope before Judson could dangle. The author wrote that the would-be lynchers were people whom he had attacked politically in one of his periodicals, and declared that Mrs. Porterfield had suffered no untoward attentions from him.

In his later years, Judson suffered from badly set bones in both legs, broken—it is said—when he was running from another woman's husband.

After marrying for the second time in New York City in 1848, Judson started a newspaper named, like an earlier magazine, *Ned Buntline's Own*, in which he promoted U.S. patriotism and editorialized against accepting further immigrants. He helped found a secret fraternity, the United Sons of America, based on these beliefs. The group eventually merged into the Native American Party—called the "Know-Nothings" because that's what members said when asked about party policies—which was devoted to preventing Catholics from holding jobs and winning public office as well as to halting immigration. The party fielded political candidates until the Civil War began.

Acting on his political beliefs, Judson helped promote the New York public meeting that turned into the Astor Place Riot in 1849. With two productions of *Othello* mounted in the city at the same time—one starring American actor Edwin Forrest and the other featuring British actor William Charles Macready—Judson and others of the "American Committee" descended on Macready's theater.

While thousands demonstrated outside, throwing bricks through the Astor Place Opera House windows and pounding on its doors, party members who had gotten inside hissed, shouted, and generally drowned out the play's first act. After the mob shifted its activities outdoors, the national guard had to assist police in restoring order. Twenty-two of the 20,000 demonstrators ended up dead in the city's worst riot to date.

Judson was recognized as a ringleader, fined $250, and sentenced to a year in the Blackwell Island prison. When released, he was greeted by supporters with a torchlight parade. He immediately set out on a national lecture tour promoting his politics and himself.

He somewhat interrupted his writing career to serve the Union army as a private from 1862 to at least the following year. After being wounded, he had his then-spouse deliver paper and pen so that he could write while recovering. The day before the war ended, Judson issued the first edition of a new periodical, but the publication soon foundered. Later, he enjoyed wearing blue army coats adorned with medals—but whether they were his own or someone else's, no one knows.

Judson toured the West between 1866 and 1868, offering lectures on temperance (while keeping up his own heavy drinking) and Americanism. He looked up Wild Bill Hickok, hoping to write a dime novel about him, but the lawman wasn't interested and gave the writer twenty-four hours to move on. Judson accidentally met Buffalo Bill Cody, went out on army scouting excursions with him, and decided that Cody was going to be his dime novel hero. The two-year trip also resulted in colorful articles about Judson's frontier travels.

After writing his Cody book as Ned Buntline, Judson turned it into an 1869 play that launched Buffalo Bill Cody's performing career: *Buffalo Bill, King of the Border Men*. In the book, a character named Wild Bill Hitchcock meets an untimely death, no doubt Judson's revenge on Hickok. After negatively reviewed but money-making performances in Chicago, the production moved on to New York. Judson wrote the first four Buffalo Bill dime novels, but the series soon was taken over by Prentiss Ingraham and others.

The cast of Ned Buntline's play Scouts of the Plains *in the 1870s: a bewigged Ned Buntline, Buffalo Bill Cody, Josephine Morlacchi as the Indian Dove Eye, and Texas Jack Omohundro. Jack and Italian-born Josephine married soon after this photograph.* MCCRACKEN RESEARCH LIBRARY, BUFFALO BILL HISTORICAL CENTER.

Four years later, Judson wrote *Scouts of the Plains,* starring Cody, Texas Jack Omohundro, and Wild Bill Hickok. Both this and the earlier play purported to tell true experiences of their stars. Judson himself appeared in the latter work's first two acts and received pans rather than praise from critics. But the ticket-buying public made these plays financial successes.

Buffalo Bill, Texas Jack, and Ned Buntline partnered to produce the 1873 *Scouts of the Plains,* but that marked the end of the Judson-Cody partnership. They had fought over division of the play's proceeds.

Judson seemed always to be scrambling to earn more money from his pen, but some early investments in Deadwood Gulch mining companies seem to have been his most profitable business venture.

Lingering effects from his various injuries helped lead to his death in 1886, at the age of sixty-five.

PRENTISS INGRAHAM
Chronicling Buffalo Bill

Prentiss Ingraham took over the Buffalo Bill Cody dime novel franchise for Beadle and Adams when Ned Buntline retired from it. He once listed six hundred novels he had written for Beadle and Adams and other publishers, but dime novel historian Albert Johannsen believed that Ingraham probably wrote more like a thousand of the books.

Unlike many dime novelists, Ingraham personally knew his subject. He had spent time with Buffalo Bull during an 1881 tour of the West, when Cody was still scouting for the U.S. Army. Three years later, he worked briefly as the advance man for Cody's Wild West show.

Like E. Z. C. Judson, Ingraham had quite an adventurous early life, but he was much better educated. Born in Natchez, Mississippi, in 1843, Ingraham attended private schools in Maryland and Mississippi. When the Civil War began, he dropped out of medical school to join the Confederates. He was wounded and captured by the Union army at one point, but he escaped.

After the war, Ingraham apparently became a mercenary soldier, fighting in Mexico, South America, Austria, Crete, Egypt, and Cuba. In London in 1869, before going to Cuba, he published some fiction. In Cuba he held commissions in both the army and navy, but he fought with rebels against the ruling Spanish and returned to the United States only after being captured, sentenced to death, and escaping.

Back in the United States in the early 1870s, Ingraham turned to writing full-time, especially for Beadle and Adams under many pen names. Not surprisingly, much of his fiction featured spies and military and seafaring men, and some of his pen names included an army or navy rank. Between 1885 and 1891, he also mounted three of his own plays. He married in 1875, and he and his wife would raise their three children in Maryland and later Chicago.

Ingraham long had worried that his Civil War wound would cause him to lose one of his feet, but in 1903 he was diagnosed with kidney disease—then completely untreatable. He spent his last months at Beauvoir Confederate Soldiers Home in Biloxi, Mississippi. The retirement home of Jefferson Davis, it had been opened the year of his diagnosis as a nursing home for Confederate veterans and their widows, the function it would serve until 1957. Prentiss Ingraham died there in 1904. ⇥

BIBLIOGRAPHY

Barra, Allen. *Inventing Wyatt Earp: His Life and Many Legends.* New York: Carroll & Graf Publishers, 1998.

Bennett, Estelline. *Old Deadwood Days.* New York: J. H. Sears & Company, 1928.

Bryant, Jerry L. "Madam of the Bulldog Ranches." *Deadwood Magazine,* Winter 2002–2003, http://www.deadwoodmagazine.com/archived-site/Archives/Girls_Bulldog.htm

Bryant, Jerry L. "Madam Mollie Johnson, Queen of the Blondes." *Deadwood Magazine,* July/August 2002, http://www.deadwood-magazine.com/archivedsite/Archives/Girls_Mollie2.htm

Carter, Robert A. *Buffalo Bill Cody: The Man Behind the Legend.* New York: John A. Wiley & Sons, Inc., 2000.

Engebretson, Doug. *Empty Saddles, Forgotten Names: Outlaws of the Black Hills and Wyoming.* Aberdeen, SD: North Plains Press, 1982.

Fielder, Mildred. *Poker Alice.* Deadwood, SD: Centennial Distributors, 1972.

Floyd, Dustin D. "Outlaws." *Deadwood Magazine,* August 2006, http://www.deadwoodmagazine.com/back_issues/article.php?read_id=133

Guern, Jeannine P. "Deadwood Dicks by the Dozen." *Deadwood Magazine,* March/April 2000, http://www.deadwooddicks.com/archivedsite/archives/legend.htm

Johannsen, Albert. *The House of Beadle and Adams and Its Dime and Nickel Novels: The Story of a Vanished Literature.* Norman: University of Oklahoma Press, 1950. http://www.ulib.niu.edu/badndp/bibindex.html, a project by Northern Illinois University Libraries.

Larson, T.A. *History of Wyoming;* 2nd ed., revised. Lincoln: University of Nebraska Press, 1978.

Lazarus, Edward. *Black Hills, White Justice: The Sioux Nation Versus the United States, 1775 to the Present.* New York: HarperCollins, 1991.

Love, Nat. *The Life and Adventures of Nat Love: Better Known in the Cattle Country as "Deadwood Dick."* Los Angeles: Wayside Press, 1907. Project Gutenberg, http://www.gutenberg.org/etext/21634

McLaird, James D. *Calamity Jane: The Woman and the Legend.* Norman: University of Oklahoma Press, 2005.

Parker, Watson. *Deadwood: The Golden Years.* Lincoln: University of Nebraska Press, 1981.

Perret, Geoffrey. "The Town That Took a Chance." *American Heritage,* May 2005, http://www.americanheritage.com/articles/magazine/ah/2005/2/2005_2_54.shtml

Rosa, Joseph G. *They Called Him Wild Bill: The Life and Adventures of James Butler Hickok.* Norman: University of Oklahoma Press, 1964.

Schell, Herbert S. *History of South Dakota;* 4th ed., revised and with a preface by John E. Miller. Pierre: South Dakota State Historical Society Press, 2004.

Spring, Agnes Wright. *The Cheyenne-Black Hills Stage and Express Routes.* Lincoln: University of Nebraska Press, 1948. Reprinted Bison Books 1967.

S.D., Trav [pseud.] *No Applause—Just Throw Money, or The Book That Made Vaudeville Famous.* New York: Faber and Faber, 2005.

Turner, Thadd. "Where Was the Trial of Jack McCall?" *The Texas Jack Scout.* Vol. XVII, No. 2. April 2002, http://www.texasjack.org/theScout/XVII.2.pdf

"The Wives and Times of Al Swearengen; Part I." *Adams Banner* Vol. 5, No. 4. (Fall 2004), http://adamsmuseumandhouse.org/images/FALL_04_WEB.pdf

Young, Harry (Sam). *Hard Knocks: A Life Story of the Vanishing West.* 1915. Reprinted with an introduction by James D. McLaird. Pierre: South Dakota State Historical Society Press, 2005.

INDEX

Italic numerals indicate illustrations.

A

Abbot, Downing & Company 7–8
Abilene, Kansas 28
acrobats 101
Alcott, Louisa May 164
Alder Gulch, Montana Territory 124
Allen, A. J. 39
Anchor City, Dakota Territory 2
Anderson, Charlie 31
Anderson, Joseph F. "White Eye" 30, 31, 126
Arikara Indians 22
Arnold, Kitty 31, 116, 126, 132
Astor Place Riot 174–175
Austin, Kitty 31, 116, 126, 132
Astor Place Riot 174-175
Ayres, Silvin Bishop "Curly" 47

B

Barnett, H. Eugene "Gene" 82
Barnett, Rose 138
Bass, Harry 95
Bass, Sam 62, 72–73
Baum, Myer. See Bummer Dan
Beadle and Adams 165, 171
Bear's Rib 20–21
Bella Union Theater 103–106, 104, 108, 142
Belle Fourche, Dakota Territory 141; bank robbery 97–98
Benham, Alex 37, 68
Bennett, Estelline 57, 58, 116, 145, 149, 151
Bennett, Granville 57, 110, 146

Bevans, Bill 65–66
Bierce, Ambrose 56–57
Big Springs, Nebraska 73
Bissonette, Joseph 114
Blackburn, Dunc 37, 66, 67–71, 115
Black Hills; expeditions into 2, 17, 19–20, 21–22
Black Hills Placer Mining Company 56
Bloxson, Mrs. 13
Bolshow, Amy. See DuFran, Dora
Bone Creek, Nebraska 91
Bordeaux Ranch 36
Borglum, Gutzon 167
Borris, Charles Henry 79, 80–81, 144
Bowman, Jack (at Six Mile Stage Station) 73–74
Bowman, John H. "Jack" (at Hat Creek Stage Station) 69–70, 73–74
Bowman, Sallie 74
Brennan, Mrs. 149
Bridger, Jim 20
brothels 12–13
Brown, H. E. "Stuttering" 46–48
Brown, Jesse 77, 84, 86
Brown, Johnny H. 143–144
Brown, Richard "Banjo Dick" 53–54
Brown, W. H. 6
Bucket of Blood Saloon (Livingston, Montana) 148
Buffalo Bill. See Cody, William F.
Buffalo Bill's Wild West and Congress of Rough Riders of the World 9–11, 158–159
Buffalo Gap, Nebraska 77

Bulldog, Madam 146–149
Bulldog Ranch 147
Bulldog Saloon 148
Bullock, Richard 166
Bullock, Seth 62, *63*, 70, 75, 84, 87, 88
Bummer Dan 51
Buntline, Ned. *See* Judson, Edward Zane Carroll
Burke, Clinton 129, 130
Burns, Johnny 117
Burrows, John 43
Butler, A. D. 9
Butte County Bank robbery 97–98

C

Calamity Jane 11, 31, 50, 63, 114, 123–132; and Dora DuFran 141; and Sam Young 53; and Wild Bill Hickok 126–127; as nurse 78; as Swearingen employee 117; daughter of 128–129, 130; dime novel character 127, 163–164, 173; grave of 131
Calgary, Alberta 94
Calhoun, James 18, 20
Calhoun, Margaret Custer 18
California Joe. *See* Milner, Moses E.
Callison, John 35
Callison, Minnie 35
Campbell, Hugh 82–84, 87
Campbell, Jack. *See* Ross, Charley
cancan dancers 101
Cannary, Cilus 124
Cannary, Elijah "Lige" 124, 128
Cannary, Lana "Lena" 124, 128
Cannary, Martha Jane. *See* Calamity Jane

Canyon Springs robbery of Monitor 79, 81, 82–89
Canyon Springs Stage Station 82–84
Carey, Charles 83–84, 87
Carr, T. Jeff 68, 81
Carson, George 34
Carver, Bill 96
Carver, W. F. 10–11
Cassidy, Butch 92, 94, 96–97
Castle, Montana 59
cats in Deadwood 120–122
Central City, Dakota Territory 2, 80
Chambers, William F. "Persimmon Bill" 44, 47
Cheyenne, Wyoming 1–2; dance halls 101–102; vigilantes 40–41, 45
Cheyenne and Black Hills Stage Company 7, 9, 15; daily service 46; offers/pays rewards 69, 88
Cheyenne River crossing robberies 61–62, 65, 68–69
Chinese community 6, 142
Chug Springs Stage Station 35, 36
Clark, Ida 105–106
Clark, Richard 166–167
Cleland, John 138
Cleveland, Dakota Territory 2
Clide, Kitty 57–58
Clough, Reverend 97
Clyde Park, Montana 148
Cochrane, John 75
Cody, William F. 29, 131, 156–159, *157*, 160–161, *176*; and Edward Judson 175–176; Deadwood Stage in wild west show 9–11, 159; dime novel character 175, 177

Coe, Phil 28
Coffey, Jules 12, 113-115
Cold Spring Ranch Stage Station 84
Cole, "Little Dick" 166
Coleman, Curly 74
Collins, Joel 62, 72–73
Collins-Bass gang 62–64, 64, 73
Connor, G. W. 56, 74
Cook, Joseph W. 1
Cooke, Ed 77
Coolidge, Calvin 167
Couk, Martin 35
Crawford, John Wallace "Captain
    Jack" 39, 159–178
Crawford, Maria Stokes 160, 162
Crazy Horse 19
Creek, Lame Johnny 77
Crook, George 13, 37, 48, 125, 158,
    160
Crook City 70
Cuny, Adolph 12, 66, 113–115
Cuny, Charles 115
Cuny, Josephine Bissonette 114,
    115
Cuny Table, South Dakota 115
Curley, Sam 58
Curry, Louis 39
Custer, Elizabeth Bacon 19
Custer, George A. 16–20, 26–27, 31,
    125, 158, 161
Custer, Tom 18, 20, 28
Custer City, Dakota Territory 2,
    42–43
Custer City Scouts 39
Custer State Park 77

D

Dakota Territory 2
Dale City, Wyoming 40
dance halls 101–102, 143

Dangerous Dick. See Davis, Dick
Davis, Dick 136, 137
Davis, Scott "Quick Shot" 37–38,
    68–69, 70–71, 82–84
Days of '76 parade 141, 155
Deadwood, Dakota Territory 64;
    cats imported 120–122;
    Chinatown 142; map of streets 3;
    town history 2–5
Deadwood Dick 127, 164, 165,
    165–167, 171, 172–173
Deadwood Theatre 49, 102, 108
Deffenbacher, Eva 149
Denny, John 37, 68–69
dime museums 129–131
dime novels 52, 127, 163–165,
    171–178
Dirty Emma 126
Dodge, Richard 53
Dodge City, Kansas 15
Donahue, Cornelius 40, 75–78
Dority, Dan 117
Dow, Georgia 122–123
Downing & Company 7
Draper, George W. 66
Duffield, Frank 152
DuFran, Dora 139–141, 140; and
    Calamity Jane 129, 141
DuFran, Joseph 139, 141
Dumont, Eleanor. See Mustache,
    Madam

E

Earp, Morgan 15
Earp, Wyatt 13–15, 14, 100
Edwards, Charlie 47
Edwards, Dolph 149
Edward VII 11
Egan, James "Teddy" 37, 48
Elephant Corral 40

Elizabethtown, Dakota Territory 2
Empire Bakery 134
Engleside, Dakota Territory 2, 34,
    127
Erb, John Jacob 146–148
Erb, Sarah Ann 146–149

F

Fanshawe, W. S. 148
faro 99–100, 132
Fergus, James 124
Fields, Samuel 34–35
5th Cavalry 27, 158
Finn, Daniel 79
Flaherty, John 79
Forbes, Lloyd 59
Fort Craig 161
Fort D. A. Russell 2, 68
Fort Fetterman 45–46; Calamity
    Jane at 125–126, 132–133
Fort Laramie 12, 20, 113, 125;
    Calamity Jane at 126
Fort Laramie Treaty 21
Fort Meade 133
Fort Riley, Kansas 26
Fort Worth, Texas 96
Foster, Stephen 102–103
Fountain City, Dakota Territory 2
Fuller, Anna 174
Furay, John B. 89, 91

G

Garrettson, Fannie 53–54
Gay, Al 59
Gay, William (Bill) 59–60, 60
Gayville, Dakota Territory 2, 59, 135
Gem Dance Hall 119
Gem Variety Theater 57, 103–106
Giles, Alanson 97–98
Gilmer, Jack 46

Gilmer, John T. (Jack) 7
Girard College 76
gold; as currency 5; Deadwood
    discovery site 64
Golden Gate, Dakota Territory 2
Goldman, Mike 74
Goodale, Almond 85
Goodale, Thomas Jefferson "Duck"
    85–86
Gore, Sir George 20–21
Gouch, Andy "Red Cloud" 82, 88
Grant, Fred 19, 20
Grant, Ulysses 19, 22
Great Northern Railway; train
    robberies 95
Green Front Theatre 129
Grimes, Lee. See Grimes, William
    "Curly"
Grimes, William "Curly" 56, 57,
    91–92
Gross, Harry 60

H

Hagers, Lew 47
Hall, James 39
Hallet, Belle 144
Halstead, Orval 76–77
Hammond, George 147–148
Harney Peak 19
Harris, Andy 40
Harris, Frank 77
Hartman, Sam 51, 66, 67
Hat Creek Stage Station 13, 37, 69,
    127
Hayes, Mrs. 149–150
Hays, Charles 66, 115
Hays, Kansas 18
Hays City, Kansas 27
Hearst, George 4
Hearst, Phoebe 4

Hearst Furniture Store 4
Hecht, Charles 74
Helena, Montana Territory 60, 108
Henry, Charles. *See* Borris, Charles
    Henry
Hickok, Wild Bill 18, 23–34, *25*, 36,
    52; and Calamity Jane 126–127,
    131; and Edward Judson 175;
    and Sam Young 32–33, 52–53;
    grave of 33, 34, 131; shooting of
    33–34, 48–49
Hickok, William 23
Higgins, Fred 138
Hill, Fannie 138–139
Hill, Galen E. "Gale" 82, 84, 148
Hill, William 138
Hole-in-the-Wall, Wyoming 94
Holladay, Ben 24
Holliday, Doc 100
Homestake Mine 4–5, 75;
    treasure wagon 83
Homestake Opera House and
    Recreational Building 4
House of Blazes 36
Howard, George "Tony Pastor" 77
Hubert, Julie 114
Huckert, George 154
Hunton, John 36
hurdy-gurdy girls 101
Hurley, John A. 75

I

Iler, Walter 62, 63–65
Ingraham, Prentiss 175, 177–178
Inter Ocean Hotel 62
Ivers, Alice. *See* Tubbs, Poker Alice

J

Jenney, William 22
Jenney expedition 22, 53

Jenney Stockade Stage Station 6, 7,
    68; stagecoach robbery at 37–38
Johannsen, Albert 171–172
John B. "Johnny" Owens 35
Johnson, Joe 91
Johnson, Mollie 133
Johnson, Rolf 54
Johnston, Mollie 109
Jones, Frank. *See* Sundance Kid
Judson, Edward Zane Carroll
    173–177, *176*

K

Kansas, Free-State Army of 24
Keating, George W. 80
Keystone Dance Hall 40
Kid Curry. *See* Harvey "Kid Curry"
    Logan
Kilpatrick, Ben "The Tall Texan" 96
King, Ella 69
Kohl, Charles 129
Kuykendall, W. L. 49

L

Lake, Agnes Thatcher 30, 32, 34
Lake, Bill 30
Lake, Stuart N. 13
Lame Johnny. *See* Donahue,
    Cornelius
Lame Johnny Creek 76
Langrishe, Jack 102, 106–109, *107*,
    121–122
Langrishe, Jeannette 106, 108, 109
Langrishe Opera House (Helena,
    Montana Territory) 108
Laramie County, Wyoming 69
Lathrop, George 36, 137
Laughlin, Maggie 151–152
Lawrence County, Dakota Territory
    69

Leach, M. F. 86
Lead, Dakota Territory 2, 4, 150
Lebby, Jim 74
Leopold, Pearl 137–138
Leroy, Kitty 58
Little Brocky 77
Little Frank (prostitute) 132–133
Livingston, Montana Territory 148
Livingstone, Henrico 145–146
Llewellyn, W. H. 56, 91
Logan, Harvey "Kid Curry" 96, 97–98
Lone Star Saloon 58
Long, Big Steve 111–113, *112*
Longabaugh, Harry. *See* Sundance Kid
Longenbaugh, George 92
Love, Alice 170
Love, Nat 166, 167–171, *168*
Love, Robert 167, 169
Lull, William "Billie" 116
Lusk, Wyoming 7, 36, 136, 137

M

McBride, Frank 87–88
McCall, Jack 33–35, 48–51
McCanles, David Colbert "Colb" 24–25
McCarty, Tom 94
McDaniels, James 108
McDonald, John 45
Macke, James 60
McKimie, Robert "Little Reddy" 62–65
McLaughlin, Archie 56, 86, 143, 145
Madden, Bert 95
mail 6; express 11–12; thefts of 89, 90
Mann, Carl 32, 49, 51
Manning, John B. 70, 84

Mansfield, William "Billy" 56, 86, 143
Manuse, Joe 56
Marble, Arthur 97
Martin, Charles 40
Massie, William R. 32, 33, 34, 48–49, 51
May, Boone 54–57, 55, 82; and Canyon Springs robbery 84, 87, 88; and Cornelius Donahue 77; and Persimmon Bill Chambers 46; and Curly Grimes 91–92; and Lurline Monte Verde 144; shooting skill 23; and Frank Towle 90; and Prescott Webb 74-75
May, Jim 54, 86
Mayo, John B. 131
Meek, Dub 35
Mellor, John 146
Merritt, Wesley 158, 160
Metz family massacre 46, 48
Middleton, Doc. *See* James M. "Doc Middleton" Riley
Middleton, George 129
Milligan, Tom 42
Milner, Moses E. 31, 50
Miner, William 82, 84
Minnie the Gambler 135
Monitor treasure coach 9, 69; robbery of 82–89
Montana City, Dakota Territory 2
Monte Verde, Lurline 79, 142–145
Monticello, Kansas 24
Moonlight, Thomas 94
Moore, Tom 77
Morgan, Charles 40–41
Morlacchi, Josephine *176*
Mother Featherlegs 135–137
Moulton, Frank 84, 87
Moulton, George B. 3

Mount Moriah Cemetery 34, 139, 141
Mount Rushmore 167
Moyer, Ace 111–113, *112*
Moyer, Con 111, *112*
Murphy, John Francis 75
Murray, J. W. 75
Murray House 138
music, popular 102–103
Mustache, Madam 100, 126, 134–135
Myers, Kate 174

N

Neill, Sue 150–151
New Bulldog Ranch 147
Newcastle, Wyoming 36
Newcom, Wirt 128
newspapers 9
Niobrara River 7
No. 10 Saloon 32–34, 48–49
Nolan, Jack 91
Northern Cheyenne Indians 19, 20, 22, 158–159

O

Oakes, Jessie 130
O'Dare, Frankie 132
O'Day, Frankie 132
O'Day, Tom 95, 97–98
Old Ironsides 9
Old Woman's Fork 90
O'Leary, Kitty 148
Oleson, Mrs. 125
Omohundro, Texas Jack 29, *176*
Oro, Dakota Territory 2
Overland Stage Lines 24
Owns The Mule 59

P

Parker, Robert Leroy. *See* Cassidy, Butch
Parrott, "Big Nose" George 89
Pastor, Tony 77
Patrick, James. *See* Ross, Charley
Patrick, Mathewson T. 7, 46, 48
Pelton, Clark 65, 66, 115
Pete's Place 149
Phillips, Josephine "Jennie" 134
Pierce, John H. "Ranger" 162
Pinkerton Detective Agency 96, 97
Pioneer Pony Express 12
Place, Etta 92, 96
Place, Harry. *See* Sundance Kid
Platte Valley Theater (Denver) 108
Pony Express 11–12
Porter's Hotel 115–116
Porterfield, Robert 174
Price, Tom 56
Prince of Wales (future Edward VII) 11
prohibition of alcohol 3
prostitution 12–13, 109; at variety theaters 116–119; terms for 109–110
Pullman, George 170
Punteney, Walt 95, 97–98

Q

Queen Victoria 11

R

Rader, Bill 60
railroads 5. *See* also Great Northern Railway, Union Pacific Railroad
Rapid City, Dakota Territory 2, 141
Raw Hide Buttes Stage Station 7, 136

Raynolds, William F. 21
Red Cloud 22
Red Cloud Indian Agency 6, 7
Red Lodge, Montana 95
Reilly, Ed 121
Rescue of the Deadwood Stage
    9–11, 159
Reynolds, Lonesome Charley 19–20
Rich, Charles 32
Riley, James M. "Doc Middleton" 91,
    92
Rosen, Fr. Peter 146
Ross, Charley 79, 81–82, 144
Running Water Stage Station 7, 12

S

St. Martin's Academy (Sturgis) 129
salamander safe 8
Salisbury, Monroe 7, 46
Sample, Billy 56, 84
schools 4, 35, 149
7th Cavalry 18, 22, 26, 158
Sexton, Inez 146
Shaughnessy, Ed 54
Shaw, Alex 43
Shepherd, Charlotte. See Mother
    Featherlegs
Sheridan, Philip H. 17
Sherman, William Tecumseh 17
Shingle, George 49, 51
Shingle-Headed Frank (prostitute)
    132
Siddons, Belle 144
Sidney, Nebraska 2, 7, 89
Simms, Annie 35
Sioux City, Iowa 2
Sioux Indians 19, 20–22
Six Mile Stage Station 12, 66
Slaughter, John 29
Slaughter, John H. "Johnny" 9,
    62–63, 64

Slaughter, John N. 62
Smith, Eugene 82–84
Smith, James L. "Whispering" 77–78
Smith, Jedediah 20
Society of Black Hills Pioneers 131
Soldier Frank (prostitute) 132
South Bend, Dakota Territory 2
South Deadwood, Deadwood Terri-
    tory 2
Spearfish, Dakota Territory 7, 138
Spears, Al 86–87
Spencer, Leonard (Len) 133–134
Spencer, Lew 133, 134
Spotted Tail 22, 59
Spotted Tail Indian Agency 6
stagecoaches 5–7, *10*; Deadwood
    Stage in Buffalo Bill's show 9–11,
    159; pictured 10
Stagecoach Museum 137
Steers, Bill 128
Steers, Jessie 128–129, 130
Strawhim, Sam 27
Sturgis, Dakota Territory 129, 133
Sundance, Wyoming Territory 7
Sundance Kid 92–98, *93*
Sunnydale, Montana Territory 148
Sutherland, Bill. See McCall, Jack
Swearingen, Al 58, 105, 116–119,
    117
Swearingen, Lemuel 116
Swearingen, Nettie 116

T

"Telegraphy" (stage passenger) 72
Tallent, Annie 104
Temple of Music 103
Ten Mile Ranch Stage Station 147
10th Cavalry 27
Terry, Alfred 158
Thayer, John 48

Thorp, Russell B. Jr. 7, 136–137
Thorp, Russell B. Sr. 7, 36
Three Mile Stage Station; prostitu-
    tion at 12–13, 36, 113–115, 125
Tid Bit (prostitute) 67
Towle, Frank K. 56, 62, 89–90
Train Robbers Syndicate 94
treasure coaches 8–9
Tubbs, Poker Alice 100, 152–155,
    153
Tubbs, Warren G. 154
Tutt, Dave 26

U

Underground Railroad 23
Union Pacific Railroad 1–2, 7;
    train robberies 73, 89, 95–98
Utter, "Colorado Charlie" 12, 29, 31,
    33, *33*, 67, 166–167
Utter, Steve 31, *33*

V

variety theaters 103–106, 118–119;
    prostitution at 104, *104*
Vestal, Madam 144
vigilantes 38–41, 45, 112, 113
Vincent, Henry "Tip" 89
Voorhees, Luke 7, 10, 46, 47–48,
    64, 86

W

waiter girls 57, 103
Wall, James 37, 65, 67–72
Ward, W. M. 84, 85–86
Warner, Matt 94

Warren, Frank 78
Warren, G. K. 21
Warren Air Force Base 2
Webb, Prescott 56, 74–75
Webster, Billy. *See* Pelton, Clark
Wells, Fargo & Company 7
Weston County, Wyoming 35
Wheeler, Alice 171
Wheeler, Edward L. 163, 171–173
White, Blanche 82
Whitfield, N. C. 88
Whoopup, Dakota Territory 2
Whoopup Canyon robbery 79–82
Wichita, Kansas 15
Widdowfield, Robert 89
Wild Bunch 92–98
Willard, A. M. 75
Williams, Bert 104
Wilson, Charley 57–58
Winchell, Newton H. 20
Winnemucca, Nevada 95
Wisdom, C. P. 56, 74–75
Woman's Dress 146

Y

Yankton, Dakota Territory 2
Yates, Frank D. 6
Yates and Company 46
Yellow Hair 159
Yellowstone National Park 130
Young, Sam 5, 32–33, 42–44, 49,
    51–53, 71–72, 122–123

Z

Zimmerman, John 90

Barbara Fifer is a freelance writer and editor in Helena, Montana. She is the author and co-author of popular histories and geographies for adults and children, including five books on the Lewis and Clark Expedition.